KIND-HEARTED COOKING

with a

30-DAY DIET PLAN

Sonia Allison

Absolute Press

First published in 1996 by Absolute Press, Scarborough House,
29 James Street West, Bath BA1 2BT, England

Cover design: Ian Middleton

Cover printed by Devenish & Company, Bath

Text printed by The Longdunn Press Ltd, Bristol

ISBN 1 899791 20 5

CONTENTS

ACKNOWLEDGEMENTS

The author would like to thank the following for their help and co-operation:

Billingtons sugars
Bottle Green cordials
Buitoni Pasta
Carapelli Tuscan olive oil
Christy hand towels
Daregal quick frozen herbs
Del Monte sorbets
Geest fruit
Le Creuset cookware
Magimix
Moulinex
Pan Salt
Prestige bakeware
Royal Greenland smoked halibut
Sacla Italian products
Schwartz herbs and spices
Swan Slow Cookers
Tate and Lyle sugar, syrup and treacle
Tefal
The Pasta Company

FOREWORD

Any diet or eating regime with too many constraints and restrictions is an immediate turn off and not something a thinking person would approach with enthusiasm, whatever the circumstances. Having been in this situation myself and been given the dreariest of diets without any redeeming features I could fathom, the monotony and boredom took hold and I vowed if ever I were in a position to remedy the situation, I would.

To succeed in doing you good, for whatever reason, eating has to equate with happiness, whether within the confines of a diet or not, and the food must tempt and tantalise, be flavourful and attractive, not too expensive, relatively easy to make and a pleasure to share, not something specifically for a dieter alone to be eaten quietly in a corner of the kitchen away from family and friends. The solitary aspect, the loneliness, the feeling of being left out in the cold are, it appears, a few of the reasons why so many dieters either give up after a few weeks or look for pastures new in the shape of a less restrictive and demanding formula, guaranteed to perform all the miracles the others didn't.

With friends who chop and change for the very reasons mentioned and with others who can't seem to cope with 'doctors orders' and turn to me for help, hoping I'll be able to come up with a magic formula to solve their dietary dilemmas, it seems like a timely and practical idea to launch my second and up-dated book of low-fat, low cholesterol recipes and tips. I'm no wizard. I can't pull rabbits out of hats. I have no mystical ability to heal the sick. But I can sympathise with the anxieties of others, appreciate the tedium of lack-lustre diets, identify with the dullness of repetitive meals and no variety. Despite falling prey to serious heart disease as a young woman, and then seeing my husband develop circulatory problems in later life, I have helped our situation along with an eating pattern packed with everything but disagreeable fat and cholesterol-laden food. We feel leaner and cleaner as a result, less stressed, not as fearful as we were and never hungry. Cures are not guaranteed but a more contented life style is! A bonus there somewhere for anyone with dubious health who wants to lose excess weight, remain a foodie and stay alive.

CANNED GOODS

These have been used in recipes through the book for several reasons: nutritional value, cost and appearance, safety and speed, convenience and availability.

For instance canned red salmon and tuna are richer in important minerals, vitamins and valuable oils than their fresh counterparts. The colour of the fish is also deeper pink and more appetising in appearance. Additionally the taste has greater depth. When the soft salmon bones are mashed into the flesh, the calcium content increases from approximately 30 mg to 260 mg per 100g. Similarly vitamin A, which in fresh salmon is 160 IU per 100g and in canned, 230. At considerably less cost than fresh salmon and tuna and with minimal waste, these canned fish represent superb value for money, are convenient to use and available nationally.

Canned tomatoes have been included where viable because they are more vividly coloured and flavourful than some of their fresh equivalents imported from European greenhouses. They are one of the most economical canned food buys and they always perform well, doubling for those luscious and ripe red tomatoes we sometimes see coming in from Italy, Spain and our own back gardens. It's worth noting that canned tomatoes contain more sodium than fresh so less salt or salt substitute is needed in the recipes.

Pulses such as peas and beans are not only inexpensive canned but come cooked and ready to use. This may sound like a lazy way out but soaking and cooking are extra kitchen chores and need time. It is also essential to know that unless pulses are boiled briskly for 10 minutes in fresh water after soaking, their natural toxicity could cause a virulent type of food poisoning – not a problem at all with the canned varieties. The only exception to the rule here is the bright orange lentil which needs no soaking or rapid boiling to render it safe. Pulses can, obviously, be home cooked but pack directions MUST be followed closely and no salt added to the water as it toughens the skin.

BRIEF HINTS

All spoon measures are level unless other directions have been given.

Use EITHER metric or Imperial measures AND NEVER mix the two in one recipe as the balance of ingredients will be thrown out completely. Cup measures refer to the North American cup which is 225ml/8 fl oz.

With oven temperatures, we all know that electric ovens work on degrees Centigrade or Fahrenheit so the little degree sign, represented by a small o, has been omitted.

Where the size/weight of an ingredient is non-critical, I haven't always been specific.

AN A TO Z OF DIETARY INFORMATION

ALCOHOL- RECOMMENDED AMOUNTS

Since the end of 1995, recommended allowances have been yo-yoing somewhat due to new research findings following studies and analyses by medical doctors and scientists into the effects of alcohol on health. The advice now is to count units on a daily basis, and not weekly as before, and the so-called 'safe' amounts have been increased to 3 to 4 units for men, 2 to 3 units for women and between 1 and 2 units once or twice weekly for pregnant women or those trying to conceive. One unit equals 1 glass of wine, $^1/_2$ pint (just over 1 cup) of beer or 1 shot of spirit. Top of the list for aiding a healthy lifestyle and reducing the risk of heart disease and cancer is wine, red for preference though white is also beneficial but to a lesser extent, provided it is drunk with food at mealtimes rather than by itself and is accompanied by water to cleanse the taste buds, refresh the mouth and quench thirst which wine doesn't do. Three glasses of water for every one glass of wine is another recommendation but if this sounds excessive, at least have one or one and a half for one. At all costs avoid bingeing and it is better to keep your drinking consistent rather than spasmodic. There is an element of confusion as to whether it is more sensible to drink for seven days a week or for only five, giving the body two days to recuperate, but overall conclusions suggest that it is more beneficial to take in moderate amounts of alcohol on a weekly basis with no breaks in between.

Australian doctors understood the benefits of wine as far back as the beginning of the nineteenth century and classed it as a medicine, recommending it for a number of bodily malfunctions prevalent at that time. Despite the progress made in modern medicine, the message remains the same almost two hundred years later and at a recent symposium on wine and health, the guest speaker, Dr Philip A Norrie from New South Wales, spent some time with me discussing this book and asked me to pass on what he considered a valuable piece of advice. "Wine in moderation* is the thinking person's health drink as it reduces your heart attack and stroke rate by half because it thins the blood, reduces your bad cholesterol (LDL), raises your good cholesterol (HDL) and inhibits oxidation."

* When asked during question time what he classed as moderate, Dr Norrie said a bottle of wine a day shared between two people.

ANTIOXIDENTS/VITAMINS A,C AND E

Vitamin A (beta-carotene),C and E act as human shields, protecting us from disease, be it the common cold or more serious complaints, and premature ageing. They are classed as antioxidents and are capable of dispersing oxygen molecules- the harmful free radicals we hear so much about -which charge round the body at the rate of knots, upsetting body chemistry and damaging cell tissues and vital organs in their wake. We need these vitamins daily.

Vitamin A

This is also known as beta-carotene or retinol, depending on which side of the family it comes from. Good sources of the vitamin are carrots and carrot juice, butter and margarine, apricots (especially dried), figs, mixed fruit salad, deep yellow tropical fruits (mango, paw-paw or papaya and peaches), prunes, broccoli,lettuce, green vegetables (particularly peas and spinach), sweet potatoes with yellow flesh and tomatoes in any shape or form. There should be no difficulty in getting adequate Vitamin A from a normal balanced diet and if you are a carrot juice enthusiast, limit yourself to no more than a wine glass a day as excesses can upset the liver. The vitamin is necessary for growth, sound night vision, healthy skin and for tissue lining the mucous membranes.

Vitamin C

Also called ascorbic acid, Vitamin C wards off colds and upper respiratory infections, helps adults to absorb the 'non haem' iron in wholegrain cereals and pulses, enables wounds to heal more readily, is a natural diuretic and antihistamine and could best be described as an antioxident with tonic qualities, protecting the body against viral and bacterial infections and the effects of antibiotics. The vitamin is sensitive to light,heat and soda, so foods with Vitamin C should be kept in the dark, never soaked for a long time in water, nor green vegetables cooked with bicarbonate of soda to keep their bright colour - they all destroy the Vitamin. Rich sources are citrus fruits, blackcurrants, rose hips, strawberries, pineapple, paw-paw or papaya, green vegetables, peppers (bell peppers),cabbage and spring greens, sprouts and to a lesser extent potatoes, radishes, spinach, tomatoes, sweet potatoes and turnips. Because the body cannot store Vitamin C, foods containing it should be eaten daily. One gram, taken every day as a supplement, will do much to assist the body's efficiency (this was recently recommended to me by a radiologist from a leading North Country hospital) and if the price of Vitamin C tablets is off-putting, settle for Linus powder, available from pharmacies. It is a concentrated form of the vitamin, very sour so should always be stirred into a small glass of sweet fruit juice and drunk with food. Follow packet directions carefully and tell your GP if you are taking a Vitamin C supplement in case it conflicts with medication like anti-coagulants (blood thinners).

Vitamin E
This Vitamin helps to stop the breakdown of polyunsaturated fats by oxygen (hence antioxident) and prevents blood clotting, muscle disorders and infertility. It also prompts wounds to heal more speedily and keeps skin and hair in good condition. It is found in bran fibre, wheatgerm, seeds like sunflower, pumpkin and sesame, eggs, mussels, oysters, canned salmon, canned sardines and tuna in oil, avocados, blackberries and cheeses. It is comparatively abundant in walnuts, almonds and hazelnuts and to a lesser extent in brazils, peanuts and peanut butter though all contain valuable amounts. There are also useful traces of the Vitamin in asparagus, broccoli, sprouts, parsley, spinach, sweet potatoes and parsnips. Safflower oil is one of the best sources of the vitamin and it is also found in oils made from olives,corn, peanuts and soya. You need approximately 100mg daily for fitness and it may be advisable to top up your dietary intake with a Vitamin E supplement. Seek advice first.

BANANAS
Contrary to popular belief, bananas are not fattening. An average-sized piece of fruit, weighing about 100g/3^1/$_2$oz, yields only 95 kcal (403kJ) , not much more than a slice of bread. They are substantial and satisfying and also an excellent source of the mineral potassium, folic acid (part of the Vitamin B group), Vitamin C and fibre. For those in high activity occupations (sports people) , bananas may be eaten on a daily basis for instant energy and to replace potassium, lost through sweat during strenuous exercise and heavy manual labour. They are at their most digestible when ripe.

CHOLESTEROL AND FATS

Cholesterol is found naturally in all body tissues and is vital in order for the nervous system to function efficiently and for the production of some essential hormones, vitamin D and bile acids. Cutting it out altogether is not a healthy option. In appearance it looks like a fatty, waxy substance which is manufactured by the liver and topped-up by dietary cholesterol derived from saturated fat. It is then circulated round the body via the blood stream. Although the liver is capable of recognising excess cholesterol and reduces the amount it produces itself in consequence, this isn't necessarily a guaranteed path to success and there are still those whose arteries and veins become furred up internally, like lime scale in a kettle, with cholesterol deposits because of an unbalanced diet, heavy in saturated fat. This results in blocked and narrowed arteries with the blood facing a kind of stop- start traffic jam. It has difficulty in flowing smoothly and evenly, forms clots, is unable to reach the brain and heart and what happens next is often a debilitating or fatal stroke or heart attack.

There are two kinds of cholesterol going round the system, often known by their initials HDL or high density lipoprotein (the good fairy) and LDL or low-density lipoprotein (the villain). LDL literally dumps excess cholesterol where you need it least (in veins and arteries), leaving it to the HDL to come to the rescue and scour it out like a saucepan brush or vacuum cleaner. It is then returned to the liver and exits the body. LDL thrives on saturated fat of animal origin such as dairy produce, lard, suet, dripping, soft margarines, Indian ghee, hard vegetable oils, fat bacon and all the fat on red meats,lamb and pork. HDL is found in polyunsaturated fats, liquid at room temperature, such as sunflower and safflower oils, corn, sesame, wheat germ and walnut oils, walnuts themselves, margarines which say 'high in polyunsaturates' on the label and fish(marine) oils grouped together under the heading Omega-3 (page 18). They are known to lower levels of LDL but, unfortu-nately, also do the same to the healthier HDL. Monounsaturated fats, conversely, have no initials to call their own but it doesn't make them any less effective in their ability not only to lower LDL but also to increase beneficial HDL. They are found in olive oil and olive oil spreads, peanut (groundnut) oil, pinenut and rapeseed oils, almonds, hazelnuts and avocados. While you are better off with polyunsaturates than you are with saturates and even better still with monounsaturates, the message has to be **cut down on your** overall fat intake, of whatever kind, and avoid palm and coconut oils often found in confectionery. As a rule of thumb, the diet should contain no more than 30% fat made up of one third saturated, one third polyunsaturated and one third monounsaturated. There are finer guidelines than this but it becomes too scientific and confusing for most of us to follow sensibly. What is important is to watch trans fats (page 17) and take in no more than 2%. Therefore always read package labels carefully.

COOKING METHODS

Almost any but avoid deep fat frying and roasting. Microwaving is superb for fish and vegetables instead of steaming, or you can use the kind of steamers listed under EQUIPMENT. Boiling is fine for root vegetables and pulses but tends to knock the guts out of lighter foods, especially green vegetables .Stir-frying and dry-frying in a non-stick pan, with a minimal amount of olive oil is acceptable. So is grilling and barbecuing, provided the food is marinated in a low-fat marinade or only lightly brushed with oil prior to and during cooking. Casseroling is another good method as it requires no additional fat and likewise stewing if the ingredients, like meat, chicken and turkey pieces, are first dry-fried in a non- stick saucepan to seal the outside surfaces and keep in the juices.

EGGS

The debate on how many we should eat weekly continues but so far the results are inconclusive. Three to four seems safe enough and consider this comment from Dr Mike Smith who is the Radio Doctor, consultant to Woman's Own and the British Egg Information Service, and also Director of Public Health. " In the past it was thought that people should limit the number of eggs they eat because of the cholesterol content of eggs. But it is now known that saturated fat- which eggs are low in - is more influential in raising blood cholesterol than dietary cholesterol itself".

EQUIPMENT CHOSEN FOR USEFULNESS

.....Electric steamers from Magimix and Tefal. Chinese style bamboo basket steamers and metal ones which fit inside

saucepans
.....Le Creuset grillet, a char-grill pan for cooking meat, poultry, fish and vegetables without fat
.....Tefal's Non-stick healthy Cooking Pan which has a sloping surface, enabling excess fat to drain away to the edges during and after cooking
.....A top notch food processor such as the Magimix or Moulinex Genius 1000
.....Hand-held electric whisks/beaters
.....A food grinder for small amounts of dry ingredients
.....A blender, the sturdier the better
.....the Swan Slow Cooker because it's convenient and running costs are low

ESSENTIAL FATTY ACIDS(EFA)
These particular fatty acids, unable to be made by the body, are necessary for the production of hormone-like prostaglandins which control the function of cells and keep the skin supple and clear. This is one of the many reasons they are used so frequently in beauty preparations. Creams containing, say, primrose oil work miracles when applied to minor skin abrasions and additional sources of EFA's are corn, soya, linseed and other vegetable oils. There are very small amounts in some animal fats (arachidonic acid). A supplement of evening primrose oil may be worth considering, so have a word with your GP or pharmacist.

FIBRE
Recently called NSP or non-starch polysaccharides, fibre comes in two parts though we tend to lump both together which is wrong in the light of modern research. Firstly there is water-soluble fibre found in oats* (the big news story some years ago) dried peas, beans, lentils and other kindred pulses, fruit and vegetables, nuts and seeds such as pumpkin and sunflower. This type of fibre lowers cholesterol levels by preventing cholesterol-packed bile salts in the digestive system from being absorbed by the large intestine. It is therefore of great benefit to anyone with circulatory disorders. Insoluble fibre, in conjunction with plenty of liquid such as water, prevents constipation. It is found in most products based on wholewheat or whole grain flour made into

bread and rolls, breakfast cereals, brown rice and brown pasta.

    * Eating oats and oat products is still considered to be one of best ways of reducing blood cholesterol and they continue to be rated highly by nutritionists. Porridge or oat muesli for breakfast is beneficial but should not have added sugar. Stir in some raisins or sultanas for added sweetness.

FREE RADICALS

see Antioxidants, Vitamins A, C and E.

FRUIT AND VEGETABLES

The Government's guidelines on healthy eating, and also those of the World Health Organisation, are aimed at urging all of us to eat more fruit and vegetables - up to 5 helpings a day or 1lb (16oz). It's not as mind blowing as it sounds at first in that the amounts can include salads, vegetables with meals, and fruit at the end or inbetween. Fruit canned in apple or natural juice can occasionally be substituted for fresh and so can frozen. Additionally drink FRESH fruit juice whenever you can in preference to sweet, fizzy drinks laced with sugar and innumerable chemical additives. To supplement or replace some of the fruit and vegetables, you can include about 25 g or 1oz (say $^1/_4$ cup) nuts or seeds in your eating plan. The difference between fresh and frozen vegetables is minimal so you can take your pick from either kind and also use canned vegetables from time to time as they are nutritionally sound and quite flavourful. A small helping of baked beans, around 2 tablespoons, is one example, as are mushy peas and red kidney beans.

GARLIC

Regarded as a blood purifier by the Ancients, we now know that a daily intake of one clove is said to lower blood pressure and also reduce the risk of blood clotting. Fresh garlic is rich in sulphur in which amino-acids and a substance called alliin are present. Through a series of chemical processes, and when once the garlic is crushed or chopped, the alliin is converted to allicin and it is this which is so beneficial to health. Unfortunately it has an anti-social odour so capsules with no after-effects may be taken if preferred, following the prescribed dosage on the container.

Cooked garlic in made up dishes loses much of its strength and potency on the breath so if you enjoy its taste to the point of addiction but resent the smell, wrap a head in baking paper (not foil as it reacts with the sulphur) , put into a lidded container and roast slowly for 45 minutes. When cooked, remove the garlic pulp and use as required. It makes an easy spread for bread or toast, pure rustic Mediterranean when topped with sliced ripe tomatoes and sprinkled with chopped fresh or frozen basil or oregano.

HYDROGENATED FAT/TRANS FATTY ACIDS

Some margarines, and other fat and oil-based spreads, are treated with hydrogen and/or hydrogenated oils during manufacture so that they are no longer liquid but set to a creamy consistency, making them usable straight from the fridge and easy to spread . When these processes take place, the end products contain trans fatty acids which behave like saturated fat (page 13) and deposit furry plaque in the veins and arteries. Because of this, you are advised to check nutrition labelling carefully and avoid margarine, cooking fats and prepared foods which show a high level of hydrogenated fat.

LIPIDS

A medical term for fat.

LOW FAT SPREADS

The safest choice for anyone trying to lose weight and also attempting to cut back on cholesterol. They are 'bulked up' with water and contain minimal amounts of hydrogenated fat and trans fatty acids (above). They really are low in fat as the labelling shows and according to a nutritional breakdown sent to me by Tesco, some spreads contain as little as 5% fat. Go for them.

MILK

The latest theory is that it is the protein called casein in all cows' milk (skimmed, semi or full cream), and dairy products made from it which is responsible for heart disease, not its saturated fat content.

The answer, it seems, is to drink goats' milk and eat goat cheese as they do in Southern Europe and the Balkans. Casein is used in the production of cheese and some plastics and is said to reduce the elasticity of blood vessels due to its homocystein content.

NUTS AND AVOCADOS
Featured on page 13, both should be eaten cautiously by slimmers as they are high in fat even though they are cholesterol-free and excellent sources of antioxidents (page 11).

OMEGA- 3 FATTY ACIDS
The explanation which follows comes from material provided by the Alaska Salmon Information Service and explains why these fats are so important in the diet. " The special ingredients in fish oil are collectively known as Omega-3 polyunsaturated fatty acids or essential fatty acids. Small amounts are found in other foods but the only one which contains them in significant quantities is oily fish. In fact fish like salmon, mackerel and herring contain up to ten times more Omega-3 unsaturated fat than white-fleshed fish. Recent medical evidence suggests that an increased intake of Omega-3 polyunsaturated fatty acids may reduce the risk of arterial blood clotting". Fish rich in these oils include also fresh water trout, sardines, pilchards, sprats, tuna and halibut. Oily fish should be eaten twice or three times a week and two more meals should be made up of good-sized portions of white fish, low in fat, versatile in cooking, easy to digest and ideal for slimmers. ALL FISH is a good source of body-building protein, vitamins and minerals but the one highest in Omega-3's is mackerel, followed by members of the herring family . To vary fish meals, canned fish is tasty and convenient, not too expensive and excellent in sandwiches and with salad. Red salmon rates more highly than pink in terms of Omega-3 oils and if tuna is chosen, it should be packed in oil, not brine, as its flesh is low in the Omega-3's. If you don't like fish, it is advisable to take fish oil supplements in the form of cod liver oil capsules. Recommended dosages are always on the bottle. If you have a strong stomach and can bear the taste, liquid cod liver oil, taken from a teaspoon, is the healthiest of all.

POLYUNSATURATED OILS IN FRYING

If these are used repeatedly for deep frying , they become hydrogenated and behave as saturated fats. The remedy is to use the
oil only two or three times before changing to fresh.

PULSES

This heading covers dried peas, the many assorted beans on the
shelves of supermarkets and ethnic food shops, and all the
coloured lentils also easily available. Before cooking, the chosen
pulse should be soaked overnight, well rinsed and, as I said in my
first book, " boiled vigorously for 10 minutes at the beginning to
prevent a rather nasty kind of food poisoning ". Exactly the same
applies five years later and the soft option is to go for canned
beans. Orange lentils, useful in soups and for making Indian
dhal, need no prior soaking and cook in about 15 to 20 minutes.

QUORN

Products made from natural quorn are a useful vegetarian option
as they are low in fat and high in what is called myco-protein.
With an equable flavour and tender texture, they have been
converted into a number of tasty ready meals by leading supermarkets such as Sainsbury's and are also available as mince or
chunks, enabling you to add your own vegetables and sauces and
create healthy main meals with minimal effort.

SALT (sodium chloride)

COMA, the Government Committee on Medical Aspects of
Food, rightly recommends that we cut down our salt intake as it
can play havoc with high blood pressure, leading to strokes and
heart attacks. As about 70% is already in the food we eat on a day
to day basis, it is advisable we use no more than $^1/_2$ to $^3/_4$ level
teaspoon in addition; we take in about three times as much as we
need as it is. Herbs, spices, fresh lemon and lime juices, English
and Continental mustards, condiments such as Worcester sauce,
Tabasco, flavoured vinegars like raspberry , together with garlic,
spring onions and chives, all enliven the food to the point where
you may find the need for a salty taste diminishes. This may take

time but it's worth persevering. Salt substitute is a fair compromise and is usually a combination of potassium chloride and sodium chloride. However, it is unsuitable for those on drugs which conserve potassium. Two things then: firstly, check medication with your GP to ensure it is safe for you to use with salt substitute; secondly don't put a salt cellar on the table. It's worth noting that Chinese food, and sometimes Japanese and Thai as well, are very salty and should be avoided by anyone with high blood pressure.

SHELLFISH

There has been some confusion over the past few years as to whether people following a low fat, low cholesterol diet should eat shell fish. The answer now is yes because it has been established that all shellfish is rich in Omega-3 essential fatty acids and the high levels of dietary cholesterol in prawns, lobster and, to a lesser extent in crab, mostly passes out of the system without being absorbed fully by the blood stream. Like all fish, shellfish are a good and nutritious protein food containing beneficial vitamins and minerals and can be eaten with pleasure but not rich sauces! Out of interest, you might like to see the dietary cholesterol content of most of the shellfish available in Britain which has been kindly passed on to me by the Edinburgh-based Seafish Industry Authority and note that the USA and Australia have taken shellfish back on board and are recommending it to those with circulatory illnesses. It seems prawns (shrimp) contain 280 mg per 100 g (3^1/$_2$oz) of dietary cholesterol and lobster lower at 110mg. Therefore if you are on a very strict low cholesterol diet, it is advisable to eat only small portions for safety. Scallops, mussels and oysters contain an average of 55mg per 100g and compare favourably with white fish like cod, plaice, haddock and coley. You will find a selection of shellfish recipes through the book, some of which have been given to me by Yvonne Coull, Head of Food Nutrition at the Seafish Industry Authority. My grateful thanks.

SMOKED FISH

There is a good variety available but it has to be borne in mind that all smoked fish is salty and should be eaten in small amounts. The cost of smoked salmon makes it viable for the

♥

occasional sandwich and likewise smoked Greenland halibut, both of which can be found in some supermarkets around the country. Smoked mackerel, peppered or plain, makes a satisfying meal with a jacket potato and an additional vegetable or salad, and if you fancy kippers, buy the undyed ones and poach them in two changes of water, starting from cold, to remove as much salt as possible. Sprinkle with lemon juice or a mild vinegar and eat with brown bread or brown toast.

STARCHY FOOD/CARBOHYDRATES

Pasta, rice, other assorted grains (see grain section), potatoes and bread are the staples in countries where heart disease and strokes are low, hence the growing interest in Mediterranean and Oriental diets. Contrary to popular belief, none of these foods is fattening, provided any sauces or accompaniments which go with them are low in fat. They are satisfying and healthy, comfort foods at their best, readily available and comparatively inexpensive. Indulge to your heart's content, simultaneously cutting back on high protein foods like red meat, pork, lamb, offal, full fat hard cheeses, rich and creamy Continental cheeses and too many eggs.

SUGAR

It is a well-known fact that too much sugar puts on weight. As weight increases, so does the risk of increased blood cholesterol levels and, as with salt, high blood pressure. Cut back is the medical message and watch out for hidden sugar in bought biscuits, cakes, sauces, ketchup, dressings, ready meals, breakfast cereals, canned and bottled fruit drinks and colas, chocolate (unless diabetic), many of the popular snack foods and shop bought desserts. You are better off doing without - bearing in mind there's plenty of natural sugar in fruit and some vegetables - or, as a last resort, using sugar substitute. The ultimate aim, of course, is to wean yourself off the craving for sweetness which can be done if you try.

TEA

Hurrah for the British cuppa! North American research has concluded that tea - be it green or black - is an antioxident (see page 11) containing polyphenols. Five cups daily not only guards against heart disease and stroke, cancer and some viral infections, but is also the equivalent of eating 2 portions of vegetables.

TOFU
A soya bean product made from curdled soy milk, tofu looks like a square of pale cheese and is fatless and almost tasteless. It is claimed to lower high levels of blood cholesterol and also increase HDL (page 11) and is a useful cooking additive in so far as it is a high protein food which is light and mild. In my first book , *The Low Cholesterol Glutton*, I wrote, " when combined with other foods, it not only takes on their flavours but also adds 'stretch', making the dish go further. It is the colour of milk, tastes deceptively rich and creamy and is widely eaten in Japan and China where the incidence of coronary heart disease and strokes is low ".

TRANS-FATTY ACIDS
See page 17.

VITAMINS
See antioxidents on page 11.

WINE
Red wine contains the chemical flavonoid which not only gives it its red colour but also acts as an antioxident and platelet inhibitor. The antioxident prevents LDL cholesterol page 13) combining with oxygen and taking on the characteristics of hydrogenated fat; the platelet inhibitor makes the blood less sticky. In simple terms,both are necessary to ease the blood flow through the circulatory system. The amount of red wine recommended is between two and three glasses daily and excess should be avoided as it could do more harm than good. Some medication and wine are incompatible and this should be checked out with your doctor.

Diet plan

Breakfasts

EVERY DAY: TEA WITH SKIMMED MILK OR LEMON, COFFEE WITH OR WITHOUT SKIMMED MILK. USE ARTIFICIAL SWEETENER

DAY 1   Beans on toast. Glass of orange juice, freshly squeezed if possible

DAY 2   Grilled tomatoes* on toast. A ripe pear or 3 large plums. * To grill tomatoes, halve 2 or 3 and sprinkle cut sides with Worcester sauce. Season with salt and pepper. Brown under the grill. Put onto 1 or 2 slices of freshly toasted wholemeal bread spread with a hint of continental mustard

DAY 3   Poached smoked haddock with brown bread. A large orange

DAY 4   Poached kipper with brown bread or rolls. Two or 3 canned peach halves in natural juice

DAY 5   Half a grapefruit with demerara sugar or artificial sweetener. Canned mushrooms, heated and drained, served with a toasted muffin spread with 1 teaspoon of low fat margarine

DAY 6   Two grilled turkey rashers * (strips) with grilled pineapple slice on toast. A large apple.* The rashers (strips) are sold as an alternative to bacon and available through supermarket chains

DAY 7   Banana 'rarebit' *. Glass of pineapple juice. * To make the 'rarebit', spread a large slice of toast with 1 coarsely mashed banana. Sprinkle with soft brown (coffee) sugar and a little powdered cinnamon. Crackle under a hot grill

DAY 8   Low fat cottage cheese thickly spread on to a slice of brown toast and topped with 2 heaped tablespoons of canned mandarins. Glass of pink grapefruit or cranberry juice

DAY 9   Low fat cheese spread on toast topped with 2 or 3 slices of beetroot and a mound of mustard and cress. Glass of carrot or sparkling grape juice

DAY 10   Toasted bap roll spread thinly with butter and sandwiched together with sliced chicken breast (packeted) and grated carrot. Glass of tomato juice

DAY 11   Kiwi fruit 'eggs'*. Bread or toast spread with fromage frais or quark. * To make the eggs, put 1 kiwi fruit into an egg cup and one in the saucer. Cut off tops and eat like eggs.

DAY 12   Scrambled or poached egg on toast. A piece of any seasonal fresh fruit to taste or a bowl of cherries or strawberries

DAY 13   Muesli with skimmed milk and 4 prunes or canned figs. Glass of grapefruit juice or a peach

DAY 14   Bowl of porridge (cooked with water) and skimmed milk. An apple or 6 dates

DAY 15   Corn or bran flakes with skimmed milk. Six dried apricots, soaked overnight in water to soften

DAY 16   Bowl of canned grapefruit. Shredded wheat with skimmed milk

DAY 17   Frosties with skimmed milk. Dessert bowl of grapes or slice of melon

DAY 18 All-bran with skimmed milk. Dessert bowl of strawberries or cherries

Be sensible about portions and keep to AVERAGE amounts. For
instance, a small can of baked beans, 3 to 4 tablespoons cottage
cheese, 2 to 3 slices of chicken, a cereal bowl of cereal and not a
large soup plate full to capacity. Be GENEROUS with skimmed
milk. As it has minimal fat but plenty of calcium, use up to 575ml
to 600ml/1 pint/2$\frac{1}{2}$ cups daily.

All the fruit given for breakfast IS IN ADDITION to any
you eat in between meals. Likewise, vegetables.

You can eat the breakfasts in any order you please,
provided they are not repeated on a daily basis. The change
round of food seems to encourage weight loss, so eat something
different each morning for 15 or 16 days then go back to the
beginning again.

Midday and Evening meals

The thirty daily menus represent a selection of recipes from the book and there are some extra ones to give you a choice. If more convenient, midday and evening meals may be switched around.

DAY 1   Midday
Mixed Fish Soup (page 53)
Tuna and cucumber brown bread sandwich OR
Cottage cheese and lettuce brown bread sandwich with slice of fresh pineapple
Apple Pie Pudding (page 200) OR
An apple

Evening
Chopstick Chicken with Bamboo Shoots (page 133) OR
Piece of Chinese roast chicken eaten cold
Quick cooking Chinese noodles
Green Bean and Water Chestnut Salad (page 234)
Canned mandarins or lychees

DAY 2   Midday
Kipper Mousse (page 79) OR
Fillet of plain or peppered smoked mackerel with jacket
        potato and a little low fat spread
Bowl of mixed salad with low fat dressing
5 dried apricots

Evening
Crab Paté (page 59) with home made bread (see bread
        section on page 205)
White Stew of Chicken with Shallots and Tarragon
        (page 128)
Baby new potatoes or Brown and Wild Rice (page 175)
Mange tout or green beans with young carrots

Pickled Peaches (page 73) OR
A large fresh peach or nectarine

DAY 3 **Midday**

Carrot Soup Tino (page 56) with wholemeal bread OR
Bagel split and spread with low fat salad dressing and
      filled with pastrami and sliced sauerkraut or
      coleslaw mixed with low fat dressing
1 slice of Prune and Banana Cake (page 216) OR
1 digestive biscuit

Evening

Red sea bream with Thai Stuffing (page 111)
Beansprout and Mushroom Salad with Lemon Grass
      (page 233)
Whole baby sweetcorn mixed with chopped chilli to
taste and low fat dressing
Jasmine rice or Chinese Noodles
Slice of honeydew melon

DAY 4 **Midday**

$1/_2$ grapefruit sprinkled with orange liqueur or maple syrup
Club Salad Sandwich (page 246) OR
Roast beef sandwich with mustard and mixed salad
Apple and Blackberry Muffin (page 223) OR
A dessert dish of jelly

Evening

Tomatoes under a Pesto Sky (page 64)
Baked Fish Steaks with Capers and Olives (page 98) OR
Fried Tuna Steak (page 104)
Mixed salad of green leaves tossed with low fat dressing
Freshly cooked tagliatelle or rice
Marsala Mulled Peaches (page 196) OR
4 fresh apricots

DAY 5   Midday
A bowl of clear chicken or beef consomme with chopped
        (minced) fresh or frozen chives
Grilled Whole Mackerel with Lime, Herbs and Garlic
        (page 100) OR
Sardines in olive oil on toast
Cut up tomatoes sprinkled with chopped (minced) basil
        and low fat dressing
A banana

Evening
Vegetable dips with Salsa (page 88)
Char-Grill Texas Chicken (page 141) eaten with
        accompaniments given in recipe OR
Jacket potatoes with herb-flavoured low fat soft cheese
Sweetcorn heated with red kidney beans and flavoured
        with a dash of Tabasco
Iced Pink Grapefruit Sundae (page 189)

DAY 6   Midday
Mediterranean Bean Salad (page 244) with Italian Bread OR
Baked beans on toast OR
Canned red salmon and cucumber brown bread sandwich
Bowl of mixed salad with low fat dressing
Slice of Honey Spice Cake (page 220)

Evening
Roast Vegetables with Raspberry Vinegar (page 62)
Chicken Tagine (page 140) with accompaniments given
        in recipe (page 178)
Fennel and Orange salad (page 241)
Lemon sorbet with kiwi fruit decoration

DAY 7   Midday
Bowl of Salmon Chowder (page 51) with French bread OR
Serving of cottage cheese with 2 canned peach halves (in
        apple or natural juice) and a crisp brown roll

Mixed salad with low fat dressing
2 shop bought plain biscuits

Evening
Risotto with Mushrooms (page 169)
Hot roast turkey in between toasted muffins spread with
    mild mustard
Salad of watercress, chopped spring onions and radicchio
    tossed with low fat dressing
Pomegranates with Flowers (page 195) OR
Sliced banana with a little 'light' creme fraîche and a
    trickle of blackcurrant syrup

DAY 8   **Midday**
Toasted crumpet spread with low fat margarine or tomato
    ketchup and topped with a poached egg OR
Egg and cress brown bread sandwich
Coconut and Lemon Bubble (page 198) OR
Mixed fruit salad

Evening
Spanish Bread (page 63)
Paella (page 114)
Mixed leafy salad with low fat dressing
Sliced oranges combined with a little clear honey and
    enough rose water to add a subtle scent

DAY 9   **Midday**
Chicken Cock-a-Leekie (page 54) with a brown roll OR
Smoked chicken or turkey breast brown bread sandwich
    with lettuce, tomato and cucumber
Scoop of very low fat ice cream

Evening
Tapenade (page 60) with either fingers of toast or cut-up
    raw vegetables
Turkey Loaf with Red Wine Sauce (page 153)

Polenta (page 176)
Broccoli
Baby beetroots (beets) heated through in fresh orange juice
Poached Pears in Grape Juice with Amaretto (page 202)

DAY 10 Midday
Glass of vegetable juice like V8
Smoked salmon brown bread sandwich OR
Brown bread sandwich made with Portuguese Piri-Piri
      Sardine Spread (page 80)
An apple

Evening
Watercress Soup (page 47)
Moules Marinière (page 112) or Somerset Moules (page
      115) OR
Greenland Halibut with Mushroom and Caper Sauce
      (page 99)
Snow Potatoes (page 68)
Spinach or sprouts
Fresh berry fruit with Raspberry Marshmallow Foam
      Sauce (page 95)

DAY 11 Midday
Glass of fresh orange juice
Extra Red Tomato Pasta with Roulé Cheese Sauce (page
      163) OR
Small portion of bought Pizza
Ice Blush Sorbet (page 188)

Evening
Ukrainian Bortsch (page 44)
Venison with Chestnuts and Whisky (page 156) OR
Crackling Drumsticks (page 134)
Baby new potatoes in their skins or Millet (page 183)
Cauliflower sprinkled with toasted almond flakes
Black Cherry and Ginger Jelly (page 201)

DAY 12 Midday
Brown bread sandwich with 2 THIN slices of half fat
cheese and chutney
A whole tomato
Piece of fresh fruit

Evening
Curried Bean Dip (page 76) with cut up celery and cucumber
Mexican Chicken Mole (page 137)
Brown and Wild Rice (page 175)
Mixed green salad to include young spinach leaves
tossed with low fat dressing
Canned low fat rice pudding (hot or cold) sprinkled with a
little low fat cocoa powder and a dusting of cinnamon

DAY 13 Midday
Dilled Salmon Paté (page 58) on brown toast OR
Brown bread sandwich with smoked mackerel, horseradish
sauce or mustard with lettuce and cress
Salad of grated carrots and a few raisins tossed with fresh
lemon juice
An orange, 2 satsumas or mandarins or 2 clementines

Evening
Casserole of Curried Chicken (page 139)
Basmati rice (page 174)
Mango chutney
Raita, made by combining yogurt with coarsely chopped
(shredded) unpeeled cucumber, a crushed garlic
clove and dash of lemon juice
Salad of sliced tomato and thinly sliced onion with low
fat dressing
Sorbet with Fruit Couli (page 93)

DAY 14 Midday
Spring Green and Tuna Dip (page 87) with fat-free
crackers like Matzos

31

Salad of sliced-up cucumber with low-fat dressing
10 walnut halves and 4 dried apricots

Evening
Turkey Cous-Cous (page 144)
Scented Fruits (page 190)

DAY 15 **Midday**
Jacket potato split and filled with low fat soft cheese
    flavoured with garlic and herbs OR
Brown bread sandwich with cottage cheese, cucumber
    and sliced radishes
Slice of Barm Brack (page 218)

Evening
Cauliflower and Roasted Pepper Soup with Ginger and
    Shallots (page 45)
Great Canton Fish (page 110)
Chinese noodles
Canned lychees or pineapple

DAY 16 **Midday**
Bulgarian Yogurt Soup (page 52) OR
Portion of Houmous
Sesame seed bread
A fresh peach or 3 apricots

Evening
Potato Gnocchi with Mushrooms and Mixed Beans (page 170)
Neapolitan Chicken (page 143)
Pasta to taste
Green bean salad with low fat dressing (added crushed
    garlic optional)
Scoop of low fat ice cream with crushed or puréed fruit

DAY 17 Midday
Shop bought rollmops or pickled herrings with
Slices of Brown Soda Bread (page 213)
A mixed salad with low fat dressing
Canned apricots or peach slices in natural or apple juice

Evening
Garden Pea and Apple Soup (page 46)
Elizabethan Chicken with Honey Cider Baste (page 126)
Buckwheat (page 181) or Millet (page 183)
Steamed or microwaved sliced courgettes (zucchini)
          tossed with chopped fresh chopped oregano
Espresso Chestnut Paté(page 194)

DAY 18 Midday
Brown bread sandwich with cottage cheese and chives
          and chopped dates
Portion of coleslaw with low fat dressing
3 to 4 fresh ripe plums

Evening
Russian Dill Blinis with Fish (page 116)
Deepest Red Fruit Salad (page 193)

DAY 19 Midday
Club Salad (page 246) OR
Roast lamb sandwich with redcurrant jelly or cranberry
          sauce and chopped Cos (Romaine) lettuce
Portion of Ogen melon, half if small

Evening
Bucatini with Mushroom and Anchovy Sauce (page 164)
Pot Chicken with Mixed Vegetables
Brown bread
Peaches and Dream Sauce (page 94) over grapefruit sorbet

DAY 20 Midday

Chicory or lettuce leaves with Sun-dried Tomato
  Dressing (page 86)
2 to 3 tablespoons of Italian Ricotta cheese
Bowl of cherries, raspberries or strawberries OR
1 large ripe pear

Evening
Spicy Vegetable Kebabs (page 228)
Chicken Tikka Masala with accompaniments as in recipe
  (page 138)
Date and Apricot Pots (page 199)

DAY 21 Midday

Pistou (page 49) with French bread
2 fresh figs or 4 dried figs

Evening
Mushroom Carnival (page 66)
Jamaican Jerk Chicken (page 142)
Polenta (page 176)
Coleslaw with low fat dressing
Palm Beach Sundae (page 189)

DAY 22 Midday

Vegetable Hot Pot
Two egg omelet
Stewed or canned prunes or 6 to 8 fleshy Californian
  ones, without stones and uncooked

Evening
Cucumber Soup with Marjoram (page 55)
Red Salmon 'Rosti' (page 118)
Beetroot and Banana Salad (page 237)
Forest Flowers (page 189)

DAY 23 Midday

Rice-stuffed Aubergines with Mixed Vegetables (page 167)
A smallish square of Feta cheese
12 green or black olives
Greek bread or rolls
Bowl of grapes

Evening

Cocktail made from cut-up oranges and pink grapefruit
with a dash of sweet sherry
Fish Gratin with Leek (page 107)
Green peas
Malt Loaf and Marmalade Pudding (page 187)

DAY 24 Midday

Terracotta Chicken Salad (page 245)
Brown rolls
Fruit jelly and low fat yogurt ice cream

Evening

Canned artichoke hearts, drained and served with Rouille
(page 81)
Seared Chicken with Green Peppercorns and Paprika
(page 129)
Rye and Fennel Bread (page 211)
Grilled tomato halves
Shop bought meringues filled with thick Greek yogurt

DAY 25 Midday

Glass of apple juice
Caesar's Scallop Salad (page 65) OR
Brown bread sandwich with prawns, low fat salad cream
and lettuce
Low fat vanilla ice cream with ginger or fruit syrup and a
sprinkling of chopped pistachios

Evening
Malaysian Mushrooms (page 65)
Turkey in the Wok with Soya Vermicelli (page 152)
Fresh or canned lychees or paw-paw (papaya) with most
of the syrup drained off

DAY 26 Midday
Smoked Haddock Fishcakes with Coriander Raita (page 105)
Indian bread
Fresh fruit salad made with cut-up oranges, chopped
stoned dates and flaked almonds

Evening
Aubergine Salad (page 236) and Cracked Wheat Salad
(page 238)
Turkey in Tomatoes (page 150)
Apple and blackberry fluffs made by folding 2 stiffly
whipped egg whites into one can of apple and
blackberry fruit pie filling.

DAY 27 Midday
Glass of tomato juice
Crab and salad sandwich OR
Prawn and salad sandwich OR
Salmon rarebit made by covering a slice of toast with
flaked cooked fresh salmon, sprinkling lightly
with 4 tablespoons grated hard cheese (half fat)
and browning under the grill.
Bowl of mixed salad
Slice of watermelon

Evening
Shop-bought Quorn Fillets or Hamburgers
Andrea's Cinnamon Swede (page 69)
Corn-on-the-cob
Sundae made from grapefruit sorbet and crushed fresh or
frozen raspberries

DAY 28 Midday

Slices of bun loaf (no more than 4) sandwiched with
Carrot Curd (page 203)
Fresh fruit salad

Evening

Chicken Under Crust (page 132)
Italian Lentil Braise (page 71)
Salad of mixed leaves with chopped spring onions and a
few unsalted peanuts tossed with low fat dressing
A small piece of Gorgonzola or other blue cheese with
low fat crispbreads

DAY 29 Midday

Glass of red grape juice
Creamy Smoked Halibut and Tarragon Spread (page 78)
on toasted rye bread OR
Peanut butter brown bread sandwich with sliced
tomatoes and cress
2 kiwi or 1 sharon fruit

Evening

Honeydew melon
Grilled or Roast Chicken sprinkled with Orange Juice
and Garlic
Cooked mixture of sweetcorn and peas
Soft fruits topped with fromage frais

DAY 30 Midday

Freshly squeezed orange or tangerine juice
Warm Pizza Style Macaroni (page 166)
Fresh passion fruit spooned over low fat ice cream OR
Slice of Nut and Raisin Cake (page 217)

Evening

Turkey Stew with Sweetcorn (page 147)

Golden Desert Sundae (page 189) OR
Small bowl of fruit and nuts

INDULGENCES AND INBETWEENS

Indulgences – daily, one only

Sweet

$^1/_2$ Mars bar (or similar)

3 squares of plain chocolate

1 cup of hot chocolate (low fat powder)

toasted teacake with low fat spread

small slice of chocolate cake

mashed banana with dash of cream

1 tub custard-style yogurt with fruit

1 chocolate brownie or brownie biscuit

2 custard cream biscuits or bourbons

1 small portion of chocolate mousse

1 Indian gulab jamun in a little syrup

1 croissant with jam or marmalade (jelly)

Stewed fruit with 2 tablespoons custard

small piece of Eastern style halva

small portion of jelly and custard

thin slice of Madeira or fruit cake

1 slice toasted bun loaf with jam

3 mint cream wafers

1 chocolate biscuit

1 jam tart

1 custard tart

thin slice of gateau

3 pieces of Turkish delight

fairly thin slice of jam roll

thin slice of cheesecake

4 marshmallows

small portion of trifle

1 plain vanila ice cream

3 tablespoons nuts and raisins

1 small chocolate eclair

small portion of fruit mousse

small piece of fruit pie

1 ring doughnut (no jam)

thin slice of ginger cake

portion of fresh fruit salad with 2 tablespoons single (coffee) cream

1 toasted crumpet with thin spread of lemon curd

Savoury

$^1/_2$ small avocado with low fat dressing

1 slice toast spread thinly with liver paté

1 packet of low salt,low fat crisps

2 crackers with small piece of cheese

3 tablespoons unsalted nuts

Small packet of garlic croutons

3 tablespoons savoury Bombay mix

3 tablespoons rice crackers

1 SMALL pork pie

8 chips

1 sausage roll

1 grilled fishcake with salad

1 grilled chipolata sausage

Small packet of tortilla chips

Small piece of pizza

Inbetweens – eat any of the following TWICE daily

$^1/_2$ grapefruit with a little honey
2 to 3 satsumas/mandarins/clementines
1 paw paw sprinkled with lemon juice
1 large peach or nectarine
10 ripe strawberries
2 slices fresh or canned pineapple
(in juice, not syrup)
125g/4oz/1 cup seedless grapes
1 sharon fruit
1 medium mango
1 kiwi fruit
1 small banana
125g/4oz/1 cup ripe gooseberries

1 pear
1 orange
1 apple
4 apricots
4 plums
125/4oz/1 cup berry fruits
1 medium slice of melon
125g/4oz/1 cup cherries
2 sticks of celery
1large piece of cucumber
2 medium raw carrots
1 medium tomato

SOUPS

Ukranian borsch

SERVES 4 TO 6

A vibrant, peasanty soup which can be eaten hot in winter with added boiled potatoes or cold in summer, each portion topped with one or two tablespoons of plain yogurt. It's an old classic, a vegetarian's delight and filling enough to sustain the mightiest of appetites.

3 medium tomatoes, blanched
2 tbsp tomato purée (paste)
450 to 500g/16oz cooked beetroot (beets)
125g/4oz white cabbage
2 medium onions
1 $\frac{1}{4}$ litres/2pt/5 cups water
2 tsp brown sugar
1 to 2 tsp salt or substitute
Juice of 1 medium lemon
1 vegetable stock cube
4 to 6 tbsp yogurt

1 Skin tomatoes and coarsely chop.
2 Put into a large saucepan with tomato purée (paste).
3 Grate (mince) beetroots (beets). Finely shred cabbage. Peel onions and chop. Add to pan with water, sugar and salt.
4 Bring to boil, lower heat and cover. Simmer 20 minutes. Add lemon juice then crumble in stock cube.
5 Continue to cook a further 15 to 20 minutes. Serve hot or cold with suggested accompaniments.

Cauliflower and roasted pepper soup with ginger and shallots

SERVES 6

Sometimes a cook - like me - stumbles on a recipe that sings out with joy and freshness, a new triumphant discovery of texture and flavour which combines East and West in perfect harmony. One such recipe is this hauntingly fragrant, golden-coloured purée soup, happy to be alive hot or cold whether garnished with chives, spring onions (scallions) or the freshest of coriander (cilantro) leaves cut into delicately thin shreds.

1 EACH medium green and yellow pepper (bell pepper)
125g/4oz shallots
450g/1lb/16oz cauliflower florets
2.5 cm/1-inch piece of fresh root ginger
575ml/1 pint/2$\frac{1}{4}$ cups water
1$\frac{1}{2}$ to 2 tsp salt or substitute
425ml/$\frac{3}{4}$ pt/2 cups skimmed milk
Juice of medium lemon
4 tsp wine vinegar

1 Wash and dry peppers. Cut each into 4 pieces, removing inside fibres and seeds. Put into a foil-lined grill pan (broiler pan), skin sides facing source of heat. Grill (broil) for 6 minutes. You'll notice the skin chars and makes crackling sounds. Remove from heat and wrap in the foil on which peppers were grilled (broiled). Leave 10 minutes, open out foil and remove pepper skins. Coarsely chop pieces of pepper.
2 Peel shallots and quarter. Put into a fairly large saucepan with the cauliflower, minus any stalks.
3 Peel ginger, thinly slice then crush through a garlic press directly into the pan. Add grilled peppers with water and salt. Bring to boil, lower heat and cover. Simmer gently for 40 minutes, stirring periodically.

4 Cool to lukewarm then blend to a smooth purée in a blender goblet. Return to a clean saucepan then gently whisk in milk, lemon juice and vinegar. Reheat briefly without boiling, stirring from time to time. Serve hot or cold in soup bowls or cups.

Garden pea and apple soup

SERVES 6 TO 8

There's a sweetness from the apples here, balanced invitingly with the other ingredients to make a fresh and delicate soup in full blown summer green.

2 medium onions
575ml/1pt/2$\frac{1}{2}$ cups skimmed milk
2 tsp salt or substitute
450g/1lb/4 cups frozen garden peas
2 medium dessert apples
575ml/1pt/2$\frac{1}{2}$ cups water
3 to 4 tbsp chopped (minced) chives

1 Peel and quarter onions then put into a fairly large saucepan with milk, salt and peas. Bring to the boil, lower heat and cover. Simmer 10 minutes.
2 Peel, core and slice apples. Add to pan, cover again and simmer a further 8 minutes.
3 Work to a fairly smooth purée in blender goblet and return to original saucepan.
4 Stir in water and reheat until soup just reaches boiling point. Add chives, stir round again and ladle into warm soup bowls.

Watercress soup

SERVES 4 TO 5

Regarded as a sophisticated soup, this one has a sparkling peppery kick-back and an appetising scent. Serve hot or cold with croutons and remember you'll need a blender for success.

225g/8oz watercress
575ml/1pt/2½ cups skimmed milk
3 tbsp dried onion flakes
1 tsp salt or substitute
3 tbsp instant mashed potato powder or 4 tbsp potato granules
275ml/½ pt/1¼ cups cold water
12 croutons

1 Remove stalky ends from watercress then wash leaves well and shake dry. Put into a fairly roomy saucepan with milk, onion flakes and salt.
2 Bring to the boil, stirring. Lower heat and cover. Simmer for 10 minutes.
3 Cool slightly. Pour into blender goblet and run machine until soup is smooth but still a little bit speckly.
4 Pour back into the original pan, add potato powder or granules and cold water then bring to the boil, stirring. Lower heat, leave uncovered and simmer 2 minutes.
5 Pour into bowls and add croutons to each.

To serve cold:
Cool down hot soup and refrigerate, covered, for about 4 to 6 hours. Stir round, ladle into bowls and sprinkle each portion lightly with grated orange peel.

Gazpacho with celery

SERVES 6 TO 7

Cool and invigorating, one of Spain's most popular exports.

400g/14oz/about 2 cups canned tomatoes
1 medium green pepper (bell pepper)
$\frac{1}{2}$ medium cucumber, peeled
1 large onion
2 large celery stalks
7 tbsp tomato purée (paste)
8 piled-up high tbsp soft brown breadcrumbs
575ml/1pt/2$\frac{1}{2}$ cups tomato juice
Salt or substitute to taste

1 Tip tomatoes into blender goblet.
2 Wash, dry and halve pepper then remove inside fibres and seeds. Cut flesh into strips and cucumber into slices. Peel onion and cut into eighths. Well-wash celery and break each stalk into short lengths. Add all four, plus purée (paste), to tomatoes in blender.
3 Run machine until ingredients form a fairly smooth purée then scrape into a large bowl. Stir in breadcrumbs followed by tomato juice. Season with salt.
4 Cover and chill several hours in the refrigerator before stirring round and serving. If liked, add 2 lemon slices and an ice cube to each portion.

Pistou

SERVES 6

France is endlessly scenic, her food a triumph of ingenuity and this Provençal soup speciality, a filling winter vegetable broth, encompasses all the warmth and vibrancy of the area. Its character intrigues and is brought about by the inclusion of basil-based pesto, a neighbouring import and condiment from Italy. The word Pistou is a corruption of pesto and is the colloquial name used locally to describe the soup.

2 medium to large onions
1 medium leek
1 tbsp extra virgin olive oil
2 large potatoes
4 medium courgettes (zucchini)
1 medium celery stalk
125g/4oz/green beans, such as snap or runner
125g/4oz/1 cup shredded white cabbage
3 medium tomatoes, blanched
850ml/1 $\frac{1}{2}$ pt/2 $\frac{3}{4}$ cups boiling water
2 to 3 tsp salt or substitute
$\frac{1}{2}$ can (original size 400g) EACH cannellini and barlotti beans
3 tbsp pesto
Pepper to taste

1 Peel onions and fairly finely chop. Trim leek, leaving on as much of the green 'skirt' as is practical. Slit from top to bottom and wash well, especially inbetween leaves where mud and grit tends to cling. Cut into thin slices.
2 Sizzle oil in large saucepan. Add onions and leek and fry gently, covered, for 10 minutes or until light golden brown.
3 Meanwhile, peel, wash and dice potatoes. Top and tail unpeeled courgettes (zucchini), rinse then thinly slice. Wash

49

celery and cut into narrow strips. Shred cabbage.

4 Top and tail beans, removing side strings if necessary. Cut into 2.5cm/1-inch lengths. Skin tomatoes and roughly chop.

5 Add all prepared vegetables to the pan with water and salt. Bring to boil, lower heat and cover. Simmer 15 minutes.

6 Add canned beans and pesto and simmer gently for a further 5 to 7 minutes. Season with pepper and adjust salt to taste.

Tips:

Leftovers freeze well in a covered container.

To use up leftover canned beans, drain, rinse and toss into green salads.

Salmon chowder

SERVES 4

Related, possibly, to Scotland's Cullen Skink - a soup based on Finnan haddock and potatoes - this North American Chowder is a variation on a Transatlantic passion, commonly made with clams and on every brunch menu I have seen from San Francisco to Orlando to Manhatten to Vermont. Clams are not exactly a British thing, so in order to keep the Chowder within the bounds of reality, canned salmon has been substituted. It seems to work.

225g/8oz celeriac
275ml/½ pt/1¼ cups boiling salted water
1 tbsp lemon juice
225g/8oz firm salad potatoes
150ml/¼ pt/⅝ cup skimmed milk
1 tsp salt or substitute
1/ tsp sugar
1 tbsp cornflour (cornstarch)
8 extra tbsp skimmed milk
1 can/212g/about 7oz/1 cup red salmon
Chopped (minced) parsley

1 Peel celeriac thickly, well-wash and cut into dice. Cook, with pan two-thirds covered, in boiling salted water and lemon juice for about 20 minutes.
2 Meanwhile, peel and wash potatoes then cut into same size dice as celeriac. Add to pan and two-thirds cover as before. Cook both vegetables together for further 12 to 14 minutes until tender.
3 Pour in milk then season to taste with salt and sugar.
4 Blend cornflour (cornstarch) smoothly with second amount of milk. Pour into pan of vegetables and cook, stirring constantly, until liquid comes to the boil and thickens. Leave over a low

heat for the time being.

5 Tip salmon into a dish and divide into flakes with a fork, discarding bones and black skin. Stir fish into soup and reheat gently until liquid begins to bubble.

6 Ladle into soup bowls and sprinkle each portion with parsley.

Bulgarian yogurt soup

SERVES 6 TO 8

A sharpish cold yogurt soup, related in part to Greek Zatziki. The garnish of walnuts is the novelty element and this typically Bulgarian soup is one of the best things that could happen to a hot summer's day.

2 large cucumbers
Salt
1 medium pickled cucumber, chopped
450g/16oz/2 cups low fat yogurt
275ml/$\frac{1}{2}$ pt/1$\frac{1}{4}$ cups skimmed milk
1 clove of garlic, peeled and crushed
2 tbsp finely chopped (minced) parsley
Strained juice of $\frac{1}{2}$ lemon
1 tbsp sifted icing (confectioner's) sugar
Ice cubes

1 Peel cucumbers then cut into wafer-thin slices and put into a flattish dish. Sprinkle with salt, cover with plate or saucepan lid and leave to stand about 30 minutes to draw out surplus water.

2 Drain well and transfer to a large mixing bowl. Stir in all remaining ingredients except ice. Cover and chill for about 3 hours.

3 Stir round, ladle into soup bowls and add 2 or 3 ice cubes to each.

Mixed fish soup with wine and potatoes

SERVES 4

A meal in itself, this is based on an old French country recipe with a nautical theme. Eat with thick slices of coarse bread, each one moistened with a trace of extra virgin olive oil.

450g/1lb/16oz potatoes
425ml/$^3/_4$pt/2 cups skimmed milk
150ml/$^1/_4$ pt/$^5/_8$ cup hot water
1$^1/_2$ tsp salt or substitute
2 tsp cornflour (cornstarch)
2 tbsp cold water
400g/14oz mixed white fish fillets, skinned
150ml/$^1/_4$ pt/$^5/_8$ cup dryish white wine
1 tsp caster (superfine) sugar
Chopped (minced) fresh coriander leaves

1 Peel and wash potatoes then coarsely grate.
2 Put into a heavy-based pan with milk, water and salt. Bring to boil, lower heat and two-thirds cover with lid. Simmer for about 10 minutes or until potatoes are soft.
3 Blend cornflour (cornstarch) smoothly with water. Stir into the potato mixture. Bring to the boil, stirring constantly, then leave over a lowish heat.
4 Wash fish and cut into cubes. Add to soup with wine and sugar. Boil briefly until fish is cooked - just 2 to 4 minutes until the raw look goes.
5 Ladle into warm soup bowls and sprinkle each with coriander.

Chicken cock-a-leekie

Serves 6

Warmth and comfort from Scotland.

4 fairly large portions of ready- prepared chicken (broilers)
575ml/1pt/2$\frac{1}{4}$ cups boiling water
1 medium-sized carrot, peeled and grated
1 medium-sized leek
3 tbsp natural brown rice
2 tbsp wild rice (optional)
1$\frac{1}{2}$ tsp salt or substitute
8 prunes without stones (pitted)
25g/1oz/1 cup parsley

1 Skin chicken, removing as much fat as possible from each portion. Put into a large saucepan with water.
2 Peel and grate carrot. Trim leek, leaving on at least 2.5cm (1-inch) of green 'skirt'. Slit and well-wash between leaves to remove mud and grit. Cut into chunks.
3 Add to pan with rice and salt, bring to the boil and cover. Lower heat and simmer for 50 minutes to 1 hour until chicken is tender.
4 Lift portions out of soup on to a board. Remove meat from bones and cut into bite-size pieces.
5 Return to pan with prunes. Bring back to a gentle boil and simmer gently, uncovered, while preparing parsley.
6 Wash well, shake dry and finely chop (mince). Ladle soup into deep warm plates or bowls and sprinkle heavily with parsley.

Cucumber soup with marjoram

SERVES 6

A surprise quality about this one, tangy yet mellow, fit for any summer's day when left long hours to chill then poured into bowls over ice cubes - one in each. It's marvellous for those who grow their own cucumbers or buy them, as we sometimes do, in street markets at low cost when there's a seasonal glut.

1 large onion
3 medium potatoes
275ml/$\frac{1}{2}$ pt/1 $\frac{1}{4}$ cups boiling water
1 $\frac{1}{2}$ to 2 tsp salt or substitute
2 large or 3 medium cucumbers
575ml/1 pt/2 $\frac{1}{4}$ cups skimmed milk
1 tbsp chopped (minced) fresh or frozen marjoram or 1 tsp dried
2 tbsp lemon juice
2 to 3 tbsp chopped (minced) chives

1 Peel onion and slice. Peel potatoes then wash and cube. Put both into a saucepan with the boiling water and salt.
2 Bring to the boil, lower heat and cover. Simmer 10 to 12 minutes or until vegetables are tender.
3 Meanwhile, peel and thickly slice cucumbers. Add to soup and continue to simmer for 10 minutes.
4 Cool soup to lukewarm then blend until smooth in blender goblet.
5 Spoon into a bowl. Whisk in milk, marjoram and lemon juice. Stir in chives then cover and chill. Stir round before serving.

Carrot soup tino

SERVES 4

Based on an Italian recipe given to me by an old friend, this is a lazy way to cook but why worry. You can drink it, chilled, from cups and enjoy instant nectar, crammed with heaven-sent goodness. For greater sustenance, eat with Continental rye bread and small helpings of ricotta.

1 can/550g/19oz carrots, whole or sliced, it makes no difference
3 heaped (heaping) tbsp sun-dried tomato purée (paste) with olive oil
330ml/11 fluid oz/1 $\frac{3}{8}$ cup lemon flavoured sparkling mineral water
$\frac{1}{4}$ tsp dried basil
Fresh basil or mint leaves to garnish
4 slices of lemon

1 Tip carrots and liquid from can into a blender goblet. Add all remaining ingredients except last two.
2 Work to a smooth purée, transfer to a bowl then cover and chill for about 3 hours.
3 Ladle into bowls and add basil or mint and a slice of lemon to each.

SIDE DISHES AND STARTERS

Dilled salmon paté

SERVES 4 TO 6

Salmon trimmings, loose from deli counters or available in packs, are the most economical way of buying smoked salmon and can easily be converted into an up-market paté like this one which also doubles as a rather smart sandwich filling with the addition of companionable cucumber.

225g/8oz smoked salmon trimmings
225g/8oz/1 cup curd cheese or low fat soft cheese
1 tbsp fresh lemon juice
15g/$\frac{1}{2}$oz /about $\frac{2}{3}$ cup chopped (minced) dill
8 spring onions (scallions)
Paprika

1 Put salmon into a blender goblet with cheese, lemon juice and dill.
2 Trim, rinse and thickly slice onions (scallions). Add to blender.
3 Run machine until mixture forms a smooth paté, speckled with green from the dill and onions.
4 Spoon into a serving dish, spread top smoothly with a knife then dust lightly with paprika. Cover and refrigerate until firm before eating.

Crab paté

SERVES 3 TO 4

A low fat paté-type spread, designed for hot toast or sandwiches.

125g/4oz/about $\frac{1}{2}$ cup EACH fresh white and dark flaked crabmeat
50g/2oz / $\frac{1}{4}$ cup low fat soft cheese with garlic and herbs
1.25 cm/ $\frac{1}{2}$-inch piece of fresh ginger, peeled and finely chopped
2 to 3 drops of Tabasco sauce

1 Beat all ingredients thoroughly together until well-mixed.
2 Mound into a serving dish and accompany with breadsticks or
   vegetable crudités.

Note
Adapted from a recipe supplied by the Sea Fish Industry
Authority of Edinburgh

Tapenade

SERVES ABOUT 6

A Provençal dip, spread, appetiser, condiment. It's earthy, sultry and bold, marvellous on rough brown bread or with dips of celery, fennel, sliced mooli (white radish), plump red radishes and thick strips of pepper (bell pepper). Use a food processor for speed or an older-fashioned pestle and mortar for mixing - either gives good results. For instant Tapenade, buy it ready-prepared in jars.

200g/7oz/1 cup tuna in olive oil
125g/4oz/²/₃ cup black olives, stoned (pitted)
4 rounded tbsp drained capers
1 tsp Continental mustard
Juice of ¹/₂ lemon
1 tsp dried Herbes de Provence
1 tbsp brandy

1 Tip all ingredients into blender goblet and run machine until they form a bitty-looking purée - not too smooth.
2 Scrape into a dish and serve as you fancy.

Tips
The Tapenade will keep fresh for about 1 week in the refrigerator if tightly covered.
If using a pestle and mortar, slice olives before mixing with the other ingredients in the mortar.

Fesulya plaki

SERVES 4 TO 6

A basic bean salad which is colourfully flavoured and common to both Turkey and Greece (where it is known as Fasoulia). It can be served as part of a meze (hors d'oeuvre selection from the Balkan area) or eaten just by itself for starters with Greek bread and a salad of lettuce, tomatoes, onions, cucumber and baby spinach leaves.

1 small red pepper (bell pepper)
Boiling water
1 can/415g/14oz/about 2 cups haricot or black eye beans
1 medium onion, peeled and grated
2 large tomatoes, blanched
2 cloves of garlic, peeled
Juice of 1 medium lemon
1 tsp caster (superfine) sugar
5 tsp extra virgin olive oil
3 tbsp chopped (minced) parsley

1　Halve and de-seed pepper then soak in boiling water for 15 minutes to soften. Drain and chop fairly finely. Transfer to a roomy bowl. Drain beans and add to pepper with onion.
2　Skin tomatoes and chop. Peel garlic and crush. Stir both into beans with all remaining ingredients.
3　Stir well to mix before spooning out on to plates.

Roast vegetables with raspberry vinegar

SERVES 4 TO 6

All the rage with followers of the Mediterranean diet and an amenable starter with crusty French bread or a few freshly cooked new potatoes, skins left on.

4 medium peppers (bell peppers) in green, red, yellow and orange
2 large aubergines (eggplant)
3 medium red onions
4 cloves of garlic
4 tbsp extra virgin olive oil
Salt or substitute to taste
1 tbsp raspberry vinegar
Fresh fennel (the herb) or rosemary

1 Wash and dry peppers. Halve each lengthwise and remove inside fibres and seeds. Cut each half into 3 elongated strips.
2 Wash and dry aubergines, top and tail then cut each into 6 thick slices.
3 Peel onions. Cut each downwards into 6 wedges. Peel garlic and thickly slice.
4 Put all the cut-up vegetables and garlic into a roasting tin. Trickle oil over the top then roast, uncovered, for 45 minutes in oven set to 200C/400F/Gas 6.
5 Cool to room temperature, transfer to a serving dish and sprinkle with salt and vinegar. Garnish with fennel or rosemary.

Spanish Bread

ALLOW 2 LARGE SLICES OF BREAD PER PERSON.

I picked up this starter idea from a family-run restaurant in the backwaters of the Costa Brava where tourists were few and far between and locals abundant. The bread, a great heap of it in a vast basket, was ordinary-looking but coarse-textured and thickly-crusted, spread with what looked like tomato ketchup and put on our table with a big carafe of local red wine. It was tough grub all round but the most acceptable part of an outdoor meal under the stars amid straying cats, hungry dogs at our feet and the odd bat zooming overhead.

8 tbsp sun dried tomato purée (paste) with olive oil
2 tbsp extra virgin olive oil
2 to 6 cloves of garlic, peeled and crushed

1 Combine all the ingredients and spread on to large and thickish slices of very fresh Continental bread.

Tomatoes under a pesto sky

SERVES 4

These smack of Southern Italy and go with almost any poultry and fish dish you can think of. As a meal opener, serve cold on a fringe of curly lettuce, three halves on a plate, a light drizzle of olive oil over each to add glisten and flavour. As a side dish, serve straight from the oven.

6 Italian plum tomatoes
25g/1oz flat parsley .
75g/3oz/1 $\frac{1}{2}$ cups soft brown breadcrumbs
1 clove of garlic
2 tbsp pesto
2 tsp balsamic vinegar
12 black olives without stones (pitted)

1　Wash and dry tomatoes. Halve lengthwise and stand in a baking tin lightly brushed with olive oil.
2　Wash parsley, pat dry with paper towels and finely chop (mince). Put into a mixing bowl with breadcrumbs then slice unpeeled garlic and crush through a garlic press over crumbs.
3　Work to a paste with the pesto and vinegar then spread equal amounts over the tomatoes.
4　Slice olives and arrange on top. Bake for 25 minutes in oven set to 190C/375F/Gas 5.

Malaysian mushrooms

SERVES 4

Fashion-conscious food in Far Eastern mood for serious gourmets. The mushrooms make a first class vegetarian main course on their own with jasmine rice or can be teamed with roasts and grills of chicken, turkey and fish. I have included brand names in this recipe as it might make some of the ingredients easier to locate in supermarkets or local speciality food shops.

2 stems of bottled lemon grass (called Thai lemon grass from Blue Dragon)
450 to 500g/1lb/16oz mixed mushrooms, including the ones with a mild
       fishy taste called oysters
1 tbsp sunflower oil
2 tbsp mild Malaysian whole seed and curry spices blend (Schwartz)
3 rounded tbsp dried onion flakes
1 tsp garlic purée (paste) from tube or jar
4 tsp fresh coriander in soybean oil (Barts)
$\frac{1}{2}$ tsp freeze dried green chilli (Barts)
Juice of 1 lemon
$\frac{1}{2}$ tsp salt
2 knobs of Chinese stem ginger in syrup
1 tbsp ginger syrup

1 Cut lemon grass across into thin slices and leave aside temporarily.
2 Trim mushrooms and wipe clean. Cut into fairly narrow strips.
3 Sizzle oil in a large frying pan. Add lemon grass, the seed and spices blend, onion flakes, garlic purée (paste), coriander and green chilli. Stir-fry over a very gentle heat for 5 minutes.
4 Gradually add mushrooms with lemon juice and salt.
5 Partially cover and fry for 5 minutes, stirring 3 or 4 times.
6 Chop up knob of ginger and stir into mushrooms with the syrup. Stir round again before serving.

Mushroom carnival

SERVES 2 TO 3

For fungi enthusiasts, the stewed baby mushrooms in a thick, creamy-textured sauce belie their simplicity and they make a superior appetiser on hot toast, between toasted muffins or on top of freshly toasted crumpets. They can also be used as a filling for jacket potatoes, tossed with pasta shells or bows, spooned over cooked millet or polenta, forked into brown rice - you name it.

1 medium to large onion
1 large red pepper (bell pepper)
2 tsp sunflower oil
250g/8 to 9oz button mushrooms
2 tbsp tomato purée (paste)
75g/3oz Philadelphia cheese with chives (light)
$\frac{1}{2}$ tsp salt or substitute

1 Peel onion and fairly finely chop. Wash and dry pepper, cut in half then remove inside fibres and seeds. Cut flesh into small cubes.
2 Sizzle oil in a heavy-based frying pan. Add onions and fry gently, turning from time to time, until light gold.Mix in peppers, cover pan and fry over medium heat fo 5 minutes, stirring twice.
3 Rinse mushrooms and wipe dry with kitchen paper towels. Add to pan, mix well with onion and pepper then lower heat and cover. Simmer slowly 6 minutes, gently shaking pan once or twice.
4 Add rest of the ingredients. Stir over a low heat until cheese melts completely and forms a sauce. Eat hot.

Paprika potatoes

SERVES 6 TO 8

Inspired by the peasant cooking of Hungary, this potato dish cooked with paprika makes a cheerful and colourful side dish, blending conveniently with fish, poultry and the occasional egg scramble or omelet. For vegetarians, eat with green beans or garden peas and low fat cottage cheese.

1 large onion
1 tbsp sunflower oil
1kg/2lb/32 to 36oz potatoes
2 tsp salt or substitute
1 tbsp paprika (sweet paprika; not hot)
2 medium green peppers (bell peppers)
3 large tomatoes, blanched
125ml/$\frac{1}{4}$ pt/$\frac{5}{8}$ cup water

1 Peel onion and finely chop or grate (mince). Transfer to a heavy-based saucepan with oil and stand over a low heat. Stir well and leave onions to fry slowly until they turn a creamy gold colour.
2 Peel and wash potatoes. Cut into dice. Add to pan with salt and paprika and stir well to mix. Cover securely and fry over a very low heat for about 20 minutes, shaking pan frequently for even distribution of paprika.
3 In between, wash and dry peppers and halve. Remove inside fibres and seeds then cut flesh into fairly narrow strips. Skin tomatoes and coarsely chop.
4 Add both to potatoes with water. Stir well to mix, re-cover and simmer gently for 15 minutes. Stir twice and eat very hot.

Snow potatoes

SERVES 3 TO 4

Creamed potatoes without butter and without cream yet as fluffy and as puffy as candy floss.

450 to 500g/1lb/16oz floury potatoes, suitable for mashing
Lightly salted water for boiling
3 tbsp low fat skimmed milk powder

1 Peel, wash and quarter potatoes then boil in the salted water until soft. Drain carefully, leaving behind 3 tablespoons of the cooking water. (DON'T strain through a colander).
2 Finely mash potatoes in the pan, working in water. Gradually beat in milk powder.
3 Stand pan over minimal heat and continue to beat until the potatoes are light, snow white and fluffy. Eat straight away.

Andrea's cinnamon swede

SERVES AT LEAST 5

A young acquaintance of mine, a local hairdresser and vegetarian, suggested mashed swede (rutabaga) with a hint of cinnamon. Heavenly, she said, and so it is with oily fish like mackerel and herring, venison, poultry or simply a dish of grilled mushrooms.

675g/1 ½ lb/24oz swede (rutabaga)
Lightly salted boiling water
2 tbsp low fat skimmed milk powder
½ tsp powdered cinnamon

1 Peel swede (rutabaga) and cut into medium-sized chunks. Put into a saucepan.
2 Cook in the boiling salted water, two-thirds covered with saucepan lid, until very soft.
3 Drain carefully, leaving behind 2 tablespoons of the cooking water. (DON'T strain through a colander). Stand pan over a low heat then finely mash swede(rutabaga).
4 Beat in milk powder and cinnamon then serve piping hot.

Puy lentils with vinegar dressing

SERVES 3 TO 4

Fashionably French, suited to all main dishes, the lentils are easily available from speciality food shops and some supermarket chains. My instructions differ a bit from those on the packs but you can follow which ever you feel most at ease with.

250g/9oz/1 ¼ cups puy lentils (brownish in colour)
Cold water

<u>Dressing</u>
3 tbsp red wine vinegar
2 tbsp olive oil
1 peeled and sliced clove of garlic
½ tsp Herbes de Provence

1 Rinse lentils and put into a saucepan
2 Add cold water until it is 1.25cm/½-inch above level of lentils.
3 Bring to the boil and boil rapidly, uncovered, for 10 minutes-essential to prevent stomach upsets.
4 Re-cover (top up) with cold water as before until it is 2.5cm/1 inch above lentils. Bring to the boil, lower heat and cover.
5 Simmer for 25 to 30 minutes until tender but still whole.
6 Drain if necessary and mix in all dressing ingredients. Toss well to mix and serve while still just warm.

Italian lentil braise

SERVES 4

A peasant dish which originated in Central Italy and now doing the rounds in notable restaurants. Serve with oily fish or poultry, or eat with rice and cooked vegetables as a non-meat main course.

350g/12oz/1½ cups no-soak brown lentils
1 medium onion
1 clove of garlic
1 tbsp extra virgin olive oil
1 tsp dried oregano or 1 tbsp fresh or frozen oregano, chopped (minced)
3 fresh sage leaves
850ml/1½ pt/3¾ cups hot water
½ tsp salt or substitute

1 Rinse lentils through a mesh sieve and thoroughly drain.
2 Meanwhile, peel onion and finely chop or grate (mince). Peel garlic and crush. Put both into a heavy-based saucepan with oil and fry gently until pale gold.
3 Add lentils with all remaining ingredients except salt. Bring to boil, lower heat and cover. Simmer for between 30 to 40 minutes until lentils are 'al dente'. Season with salt and serve hot.

Vegetable hot-pot

SERVES 6

With origins in Bulgaria where it is called Guvetch, this is the Balkan answer to Ratatouille and perfect steaming hot with polenta or pasta. It's also appetising cold with yesterday's brown rice and goes well with smoked mackerel and other oily fish.

3 cloves of garlic
2 medium onions
4 medium courgettes (zucchini)
225g/8oz fresh green beans
1 EACH medium red and green pepper (bell peppers)
6 medium tomatoes, blanched
1 fairly small red chilli, slit and seeds removed
1 tbsp extra virgin olive oil
1 $\frac{1}{2}$ pinches of salt or substitute

1 Peel garlic and slice. Peel onions and very thinly slice. Wash and dry courgettes (zucchini), top and tail then cut into thickish slices. Wash beans, top and tail and cut into chunks.
2 Wash peppers, cut each in half then remove inside fibres and seeds. Cut flesh into strips.
3 Skin tomatoes and coarsely chop. Cut chilli into narrow strips. Wash hands immediately as the chilli juices can sting and burn, especially if in contact with lips and eyes.
4 Heat oil in a large and heavy-based pan. As soon as it is hot and sizzling, add all the prepared vegetables and chilli.
5 Bring to the boil, stirring. Season with salt, lower heat and cover. Simmer 45 minutes, allowing mixture to bubble gently but not boil ferociously. Stir several times.

'Pickled' Peaches

SERVES 6 TO 8

Be it Christmas, Easter or just a weekend that's special, eat whatever you've roasted with this boozy, out-of-the-ordinary pickle. Not only is it a pretty colour, it is also tart, smart and unexpectedly sophisticated.

3 large ripe peaches
Boiling water
3 tbsp marsala or sweet sherry
Grated peel and juice of $\frac{1}{2}$ washed lime
$2\frac{1}{2}$ tbsp light brown muscovado sugar
1 star anise
$\frac{1}{2}$ tbsp cornflour (cornstarch)
4 tbsp cold water
$\frac{1}{2}$ tsp vanilla essence (extract)
$\frac{1}{2}$ tsp Worcestershire sauce

1 Put peaches into a bowl and cover with boiling water. Leave to stand for 3 minutes.Drain and rinse under cold water then peel with the help of a stainless knife. Cut each peach in half, remove stones then slice flesh as you would an apple.
2 Pour marsala or sherry into a heavy-based saucepan then add the lime peel and juice with sugar and star anise.
3 Bring to the boil and bubble fairly briskly for 2 minutes. Gently mix in the peach slices.
4 To finish, mix cornflour (cornstarch) smoothly with water then add vanilla and sauce. Carefully mix into peaches and boil gently until mixture thickens, stirring all the time.
5 Simmer 2 minutes, transfer to a bowl and serve warm or just cold.

To keep:
Cover leftovers and keep refrigerated up to a week

Dips, Spreads, Sauces and Dressings

Curried bean dip

SERVES 8

A stunner without effort. Serve with cut-up vegetables, pieces of warm Middle Eastern bread or use as a curry accompaniment in place of yogurt.

1 can/14oz/400g/2 cups curried chick peas (garbanzos), from Oriental
　　food stores
1 clove of garlic, peeled and sliced
$\frac{1}{2}$ tsp cinnamon
1 tsp ground cummin
2 tsp sunflower or groundnut (peanut) oil
Juice of $\frac{1}{2}$ medium lemon
3 tsp chopped coriander (cilantro) in soybean oil, sold in jars
Extra fresh coriander (cilantro) leaves for garnishing

1　Drain chick peas (garbanzos) and transfer to food processor bowl.
2　Add all remaining ingredients and work to a smooth purée.
3　Scrape into a serving bowl or dish and garnish with sprays of fresh coriander.

Tip:
Drained liquid from the chick peas can be treated as stock and used in curries.

Houmous

SERVES 4 TO 6

Greek and Middle Eastern, Houmous is a nutritious and aromatic dip which can also double as a spread. Pack into warm Pitta bread with mixed salad for an Israeli-style snack. Eat with vegetable crudites. Thin down a little with hot water and use as a salad dressing in place of mayonnaise.

1 can/440g/15oz/2 cups chick peas (garbanzos) in water
175g/6oz/about $^3/_4$ cup tahini (sesame seed paste), available in jars
1 to 2 cloves of garlic, peeled and sliced
Juice of 1 large lemon

1 Put chick peas (garbanzos) and liquid from can into blender goblet.
2 Well stir tahini to distribute the oil and add to blender with all remaining ingredients. Run machine until mixture forms a thickish paste.
3 Thin down with a few tablespoons of hot water if too dense for personal taste.

Creamy smoked halibut and tarragon spread

SERVES 4

A healthy extravagance and outstandingly good on hot toast, toasted crumpets and inside jacket potatoes. It also makes an unusual sandwich filling.

8 leaves of fresh tarragon
125g/4oz/$\frac{1}{2}$ cup Philadelphia cheese (light)
100g/3$\frac{1}{2}$ oz smoked halibut
Juice of $\frac{1}{2}$ large lemon
Cayenne pepper to taste

1 Wash tarragon and dry between paper towels.
2 Put into a food processor with all remaining ingredients and blend until smooth.
3 Transfer to a serving dish and eat as suggested, covering and refrigerating leftovers up to 3 days.

Kipper mouse

SERVES 4 TO 5

Use vacuum packs of cooked kipper fillets for this one to halt strong smells taking over the kitchen or use the old-fashioned method of 'jugging' to cook small kippers. Put into a fairly large glass or enamel jug, cover with boiling water and leave to stand between 5 and 7 minutes with a saucer or small plate on top. Drain and use. The choice of German quark in the recipe is deliberate in that it is totally bland and counteracts the saltiness of the fish.

225g to 250g/8oz pack of cooked kipper fillets
250g/8oz/1 $^1/_8$ cup very low fat quark
Juice of 1 medium lemon
1 tsp English mustard powder
1 white from large egg

1 Skin kipper fillets and mash <u>finely</u> in a bowl.
2 Gradually beat in quark. When evenly-combined and as smooth as you can get the mixture without a blender or food processor, work in lemon juice and mustard.
3 Beat egg white to a stiff snow and fold gently into kipper paste.
4 Spoon into a serving dish and eat with fingers of hot brown toast.

<u>Tip:</u>
Cover leftovers and refrigerate up to 2 days.

Portuguese piri-piri sardine spread

Serves 2 to 3

A hasty spread with a dash of fire.

1 can (120 g or 3 $\frac{1}{2}$ oz) sardines in olive oil
2 tbsp dried tomato purée or pâté (paste) in olive oil (shop bought)
1 clove of garlic
1 tsp piri-piri seasoning
Salt or substitute to taste

1 Mash sardines and their oil finely together. Add the tomato.
2 Peel garlic and crush in through a garlic press. Add piri-piri
   seasoning. Mix thoroughly, seasoning to taste with salt.

Rouille

SERVES 4 TO 6

A punchy French condiment/sauce with fire in its belly, intended to be dolloped from spoons into fish soup like the classic Provençal Bouillabaisse, though it takes just as happily to other, simpler marine brews. It resembles a thickish mayonnaise and contains breadcrumbs, in common with Greek Skordalia and French Aioli as they used to make in the old days by purists. A chancy and impulsive thing to do was to use Roulé light cheese as the main ingredient but the experiment paid off handsomely and the result was first-rate.

1 plump red chilli
3 garlic cloves, peeled and sliced
4 tsp extra virgin olive oil
100g/3 $\frac{1}{2}$ oz Roulé light cheese with herbs and garlic
3 tbsp skimmed milk
4 tbsp soft breadcrumbs, white or brown

1 Halve chilli, remove seeds and cut flesh into pieces. Immediately wash your hands as chilli remnants on the skin can cause burning.
2 Put into a food processor or blender goblet with all remaining ingredients.
3 Run machine until mixture becomes the consistency of mayonnaise but marginally less smooth because of the crumbs.
4 Use as suggested in the short introduction. Cover leftovers and refrigerate up to 4 days.

Spaghetti sauce without meat

SERVES 6

Aubergines (eggplant) are sometimes known as 'poor man's caviar', a quality vegetable which makes an ingenious substitute for beef. This robust Spag Bol sauce proves the point and if you want to ring the changes altogether, skip the spaghetti and try it with brown rice, polenta, cous-cous, buckwheat or millet.

3 medium onions
2 medium carrots
1 medium leek
2 cloves of garlic
1 tbsp olive or sunflower oil
3 medium aubergines (eggplant)
4 medium tomatoes, blanched
12 cup mushrooms
1 tsp brown sugar
2 tsp salt or substitute
225ml/8 fluid oz/1 cup water
4 tbsp tomato purée (paste)

1 Peel then finely grate onions and carrots. Tip into a large saucepan. Slit leek, wash well between the leaves to remove earth and grit then cut into thin slices. Add to pan.
2 Peel and crush in the garlic. Stir in oil. Stir-fry over a moderate heat for 10 minutes or so until lightly-browned.
3 Meanwhile, peel and chop aubergines (eggplant). Skin tomatoes and chop. Trim mushrooms and also chop. Add all three vegetables to pan with rest of ingredients.
4 Bring to the boil, lower heat and cover. Simmer for 12 minutes, stirring a few times.
5 Serve in any way you please.

Polish dill sauce

SERVES 4

*We first came upon this incredibly light and refined sauce in our favourite
Polish restaurant, Zamoyski, in London's trendy Hampstead. Icy vodka of
every persuasion, including Passover vodka, was readily to hand, brightly-
coloured candles flickered on the closely-knit tables and live entertainment -
balalikas, violins and throbbing voices - recalled sentimental Middle European
and Russian songs from days long gone by. The food was infinitely more quiet
and digestible and the Dill Sauce below was designed exclusively for meat loaf,
or Klops in Polish, which two of us chose as a main course. When I made the
sauce some time later at home, I gave the meat loaf a miss and served poached
salmon instead. The combination of tastes was memorable and the sauce is not
to be missed.*

1 vegetable stock cube (the best for this is Telma)
275ml/$\frac{1}{2}$ pt/1 $\frac{1}{4}$ cups warm water
1 tbsp cornflour
6 to 8 tbsp finely chopped (minced) dill
4 tbsp Greek style yogurt or low fat set yogurt
Salt to taste

1 Crumble stock cube into the measured amount of water and
   pour into a saucepan.
2 Sprinkle in cornflour. Stir over a low heat until smooth then,
   still stirring, bring to the boil. Lower heat.
3 Stir in dill and yogurt, season with salt and reheat gently
   without boiling.

♥

Gado-Gado sauce

SERVES 4 TO 6

Gado-Gado sauce is authentically Indonesian and contains one of the country's most widely used ingredients - peanuts or, in this case, peanut butter. The version here was devised by Schwartz, of herb and spice fame, and the only amendment made by me was to use canned coconut instead of high-fat creamed coconut.

2 tsp peanut (groundnut) oil
$\frac{1}{2}$ tsp EACH ground ginger and mild chilli powder or crushed chillies
1 tsp light brown soft sugar
275ml/$\frac{1}{2}$ pt/1$\frac{1}{4}$ cups canned coconut milk
$\frac{1}{4}$ tsp salt or substitute
2 tsp lemon juice

1 Heat oil in a saucepan and add the ginger, chilli powder or crushed chillies and peanut butter. Cook, stirring, for 1 minute.
2 Remove from heat and stir in all remaining ingredients.
3 Simmer gently for about 5 minutes until the sauce is smooth and creamy. If it's too thick for personal taste, thin down with a little boiling water. Serve with cooked vegetables or a mixed salad.

Mediterranean vegetable sauce

SERVES 4 TO 6

You can serve this chunky sauce with almost anything - pasta, rice, cous-cous, barley, poultry and fish. It's laden with vegetables, containing all the things to make it nutritionally worthwhile and tastes of golden holidays abroad.

5 heaped tbsp dried onions
1 tbsp olive oil
6oz/175g/1 cup washed and thinly sliced celery
2 medium red or orange peppers (bell peppers)
450g/1lb/16oz ripe tomatoes, blanched
500g/1lb 2oz/2$\frac{3}{8}$ cup passata (sieved tomatoes)
2 tsp caster sugar
2 tbsp chopped fresh mixed herbs or 1 tsp dried Italian seasoning

1 Put the onions and oil into a large and heavy-based saucepan.
2 Add celery. Fry gently until pale gold, stirring frequently.
3 Meanwhile wash and dry peppers. Halve, remove inside fibres and seeds and cut flesh into narrow strips. Blanch tomatoes then skin and chop. Add both to pan with passata and sugar.
4 Bring to the boil, stirring. Lower heat and cover. Simmer for 30 minutes. Mix in herbs or seasoning.

Tip:
Sauce freezes well.

Sun-dried tomato dressing

SERVES 4 TO 6

Sun-dried tomatoes have been done to death by food gurus and become something of a bore in consequence but used in this speckly red dressing with lemonade - something I've never come across before - they're a triumph. Spoon the dressing over salads, mix it with about six tablespoons of thick yogurt to make a dip, or combine it with thinly sliced mushrooms for a slightly eccentric starter. It's a talking point, whichever way you use it.

10 pieces of bottled sun-dried tomatoes in olive oil, drained
2 cloves of garlic, peeled
2 tbsp oil from tomatoes
2 tbsp Balsamic vinegar
1 tbsp Japanese Teriyaki sauce
Juice of $\frac{1}{2}$ lemon, strained
2 fluid oz/50ml/$\frac{1}{4}$ cup sparkling lemonade

1 Crush down the dried tomatoes in a mini blender or a hand-held blender fitted with a small S-shaped metal blade.
2 Put into a bowl, crush in the garlic through a garlic press then beat in all remaining ingredients.

A note on Balsamic vinegar:
An Italian technique of making vinegar from sweet Trebbiano grapes which dates back about 800 years. It is produced in the Modena region of the country and aged slowly in large wooden barrels. The result is a dark brown, rich-tasting and slightly sweet acidic vinegar without too much sharpness. It is denser than malt and wine vinegars and a superior additive to dressings, bastes and marinades. Avoid using it on green salads with a high proportion of lettuce as it darkens the leaves.

Mushrooms in tomato dressing

SERVES 6

Thinly slice 450g to 500g (1lb or ½ kg) medium-sized cup mushrooms, first trimmed and rinsed. Put into a bowl and toss with the sun-dried tomato dressing (page 86). Spoon equally into 6 smallish dishes and garnish each with a wedge of orange and 1 or 2 fresh basil leaves.

Spring green and tuna dip

SERVES 4 TO 5

A tasteful blend of flavours provides an appetising backdrop for dunks of cut-up fresh pineapple, plump spring onions and button mushrooms.

1 can/185 to 200g/7oz/1 cup tuna in oil
200g/7oz/1 cup thick set yogurt
1 tsp Continental mustard
4 tbsp finely chopped (minced) dill
Strained juice of ½ lemon

1 Tip tuna and its oil into a bowl and mash down finely with a fork.
2 Beat in yogurt then stir in all remaining ingredients.
3 Transfer to a serving dish before eating.

Salsa

SERVES 6

A Mexican style condiment, a cold sauce with an edge, fiery, zippy, trendy. Eat it with chilli con anything, cut-up vegetables as a starter, cold roast poultry, even a once-a-week omelet. It mellows gracefully on standing and keeps in the cool, covered, for about 5 days.

1 or 2 cloves of garlic
1 fairly large Spanish onion
1 large green chilli
4 medium tomatoes, blanched
3 tbsp fresh coriander (cilantro)
1 tsp salt or substitute
2 tsp olive oil

1 Peel garlic and crush into a mixing bowl through a garlic press. Finely grate onion and add.
2 Slit chilli and remove seeds. Finely chop flesh and add to garlic and onion. Wash hands immediately as chilli residue can burn the skin and is dangerous if it gets near eyes.
3 Skin tomatoes and finely chop. Rinse and dry coriander (cilantro) leaves and also chop (mince). Add both to garlic mixture with salt and oil. Stir well until thoroughly combined.

Creamy carrot sauce

SERVES 4

A fine specimen of a high-speed sauce, coloured apricot and creamy-textured, open to any reasonable suggestion. For intance, it goes beautifully with fish and poultry, is something special over green vegetables and makes an entertaining sauce for prettily-shaped pasta like bells and bows.

1 large can whole carrots (550 g or 20oz)
1 clove of garlic, peeled
125g/4oz/$^1/_2$ cup low fat thick yogurt
$^1/_2$ tsp salt or substitute
2 tbsp chopped (minced) fresh mixed herbs, or use frozen if more
        convenient
3 tbsp carrot liquid from can
Juice of $^1/_2$ lime
2 tsp light muscovado sugar

1 Drain carrots, reserving liquid from can and use in soups, sauces and stews. Work carrots to a purée in a blender or by mashing down finely with a fork.
2 Scrape into a saucepan. Crush in garlic then add all remaining ingredients.
3 Bring to the boil, lower heat and two-thirds cover. Simmer for 5 minutes over a low heat before serving.

Jungle pepper sauce

SERVES 4 TO 5

Modernistic and smartly turned-out, use this piquantly sweet-sour and flame-coloured sauce as a dressing for hot new potatoes, toss it into a beany salad, spoon it over cold chicken, combine it with a cubed beetroot and sliced onion salad for a startling colour effect and off-beat taste.

1 jar or can (about 320 g or 11oz) whole sweet red peppers (pimientos) in brine
1 tsp Worcester sauce
1 tbsp fresh lime juice
1 tsp onion salt
100g/3 $\frac{1}{2}$ oz/ about $\frac{1}{2}$ cup fromage frais, either plain or with garlic and herbs, at kitchen temperature

1 Purée the peppers and their liquid in a blender with the Worcester sauce, lime juice and onion salt.
2 In separate bowl, beat fromage frais until softened.
3 Gradually beat in pepper mixture and continue to beat until sauce is absolutely smooth.
4 Store up to 5 days in an airtight container in the refrigerator.

Oriental sauce express

SERVES 4 TO 5

A lucious, fruity sauce, made in no time and well suited to roast or grilled chicken or turkey. It's sort of Chinesey - or a Western relation.

2 thickish slices of fresh peeled pineapple or 3 slices of canned in juice
1 $\frac{1}{2}$ tbsp cornflour (cornstarch)
275ml/$\frac{1}{2}$ pt/1 $\frac{1}{4}$ cups cold water
1 vegetable stock cube
2 tsp dried mixed pepper flakes
1 tbsp soy sauce
2 tbsp malt vinegar
1 tbsp caster sugar
$\frac{1}{4}$ tsp 5-spice powder

1 Chop up pineapple coarsely, removing central hard core if necessary.
2 Tip cornflour (cornstarch) into a small saucepan. Gradually blend in water then crumble in stock cube between fingers. Add pepper flakes.
3 Bring to the boil, stirring constantly. As soon as sauce has thickened, stir in pineapple with all remaining ingredients.
4 Heat through and serve.

Brown breadcrumb sauce with herbs

SERVES 6 TO 8

A natural choice to accompany grilled and roast poultry, particularly at Christmas.

275ml/½ pt/1¼ cups skimmed milk
2 tbsp water
1 medium onion, peeled
1 bouquet garni sachet (shop bought)
50g/2oz/1 cup soft brown breadcrumbs
Salt and pepper to taste
1 tbsp chopped (minced) chives
1 tbsp chopped (minced) parsley
½ tsp finely grated lemon peel

1 Put milk and water into a saucepan. Add onion and bouquet garni sachet.
2 Bring just up to the boil, switch off heat and cover. Leave to stand for 30 minutes for flavours to meld.
3 Strain milk into a clean pan and stand over a low heat. Stir in breadcrumbs and continue to simmer gently until sauce is thick and smooth.
4 Season to taste with salt and pepper then stir in rest of ingredients. Serve hot.

Fruit coulis

SERVES ABOUT 4

A clear, glossy sauce used by leading chefs for top drawer desserts. It can go over or under a whatever it is you are serving and looks fabulous intertwined with sorbet in sundae glasses.

350g/12oz/3 cups raspberries or mixture of red berry fruits
3 tbsp caster (superfine) sugar
1 tbsp cornflour (cornstarch)
5 tbsp cold water
1 tsp vanilla essence (extract)
1 tsp lemon juice

1 Gently rinse berries then rub through a fine mesh sieve into an enamel or stainless steel pan.
2 Stir in sugar. Blend cornflour (cornstarch) to a smooth liquid with the water. Add to berries.
3 Cook, stirring constantly, until coulis comes to the boil and thickens. At this stage it should look crystal clear.
4 Stir in last 2 ingredients, cover to keep out dust and leave until cold before using.

Peaches and dream sauce

SERVES 6

One hot Saturday afternoon in July last year, my local greengrocer offered me a box of fully ripe peaches for a song. Unable to resist a bargain, I bought the lot and turned most of them into this sweet-scented sauce which brought summer into our lives all year long. It's glorious warm over Honey Spice Cake (page 220), used as a topping or sorbet and, if you appreciate sweet and savoury foods together, with roast turkey at Christmas instead of the more usual cranberry sauce.

6 large ripe peaches
75g/3oz/$^3/_8$ cup caster (superfine) sugar
50ml/2 fluid oz/$^1/_4$ cup water
1 $^1/_2$ tbsp cornflour (cornstarch)
2 tbsp lemon juice
1 extra tbsp cold water
1 $^1/_2$ tsp vanilla essence (extract)

1 Put peaches into a deep bowl and cover with boiling water. Leave to stand for 5 minutes, rotating them once with a spoon. Drain.
2 Cover with cold water and leave for 10 minutes. Drain again and slide off skins.
3 Halve peaches, twist apart and remove stones. Cut flesh into slices and leave aside for the time being.
4 Meanwhile tip sugar and first amount of water into a saucepan. Stir over a low heat until sugar dissolves. Add peach slices and cook 3 minutes.
5 Mix cornflour (cornstarch) smoothly with lemon juice and extra water. Mix into peaches then cook gently, stirring, until sauce comes to the boil and thickens. Simmer 2 minutes, stir in vanilla and serve warm or cold.

Tip:
To keep for Christmas, freeze in covered containers.

Raspberry marshmallow foam sauce

SERVES 4 TO 6

A fast, fluffy sauce with a whisper of sharpness. It does wonders to a rice or semolina (cream of wheat) pudding and is magic as a topping for sliced bananas, rings of fresh pineappple or a fresh fruit salad. It also has a cheering effect on low fat ice cream.

25g/8oz/2 cups fresh raspberrries
$\frac{1}{2}$ jar/about $\frac{1}{2}$ cup marshmallow fluff

1 Crush raspberries into a mixing bowl.
2 Gradually whisk in the marshmallow fluff. Use straight away.

FISH

Baked fish steaks with capers and olives

SERVES 4

With a hint of Southern Europe, the fish steaks have a forceful personality, best eaten with rice, tagliatelli or thick slices of country brown bread.

4 fish steaks: cod, salmon or haddock
1 large onion
1 small head of fennel
1 tbsp fresh lemon juice
12 stoned (pitted) black olives, sliced
1 tbsp drained capers
1 tbsp chopped (minced) fresh or frozen basil
4 medium tomatoes, blanched and skinned
2 tsp light muscovado sugar
$\frac{1}{2}$ to 1 tsp salt or substitute

1 Set oven to 180C/350F/Gas 4. Lightly oil a fairly shallow heatproof dish.
2 Wash fish and arrange in a single layer in prepared dish.
3 Peel and grate onion. Trim fennel and grate. Put both into a mixing bowl.
4 Add lemon juice, olives, capers and basil. Chop tomatoes and stir in with sugar and salt.
5 Spoon over fish, cover with oiled foil and bake for 35 minutes.

Greenland halibut with mushroom and caper sauce

SERVES 4

This is a mild and delicate fish, different in character entirely from the halibut we're used to, mostly sold frozen but occasionally found fresh on the slab as we discovered to our surprise in Leicester market. It's a lively hive of activity there, well worth a visit, where knowledgeable vendors are only too glad to explain the history, geography and idiosyncrasies of each variety of artistically laid-out fish.

175g/6oz cup mushrooms
1kg/2lb Greenland halibut fillet
275ml/$\frac{1}{2}$ pt/1$\frac{1}{4}$ cups skimmed milk
1$\frac{1}{2}$ tbsp cornflour (cornstarch)
3 tbsp cold water
3 tbsp drained capers
1 tsp salt or substitute
4 tbsp very low fat fromage frais or quark
1 tsp Continental mustard
Fresh coriander for garnishing

1 Trim mushrooms then wipe clean and roughly chop.
2 Wash and dry halibut, cut into 4 portions and transfer to a grill pan lined with lightly oiled foil. Grill 10 minutes, carefully turning once and keeping pan about 10cm/4-inches below source of heat.
3 Meanwhile, put mushrooms and milk into saucepan and bring to the boil. Simmer for 3 minutes.
4 Mix cornflour (cornstarch) smoothly with water. Add to mushrooms and milk with capers and salt. Bring to the boil, stirring all the time.
5 Simmer gently for 2 minutes. Mix in fromage frais or quark and mustard then heat through for a further minute.
6 Arrange the fish on 4 warm plates and coat with the hot sauce. Garnish with coriander.

Grilled whole mackerel with lime, herbs and garlic

SERVES 2

If you were served up with something like this on holiday under a Mediterranean, Aegean or Adriatic sky, a carafe of wine and basket of bread to hand and a candle on the table lighting up the scene, you'd pay no small sum for the privilege and come home enthusiastically extolling the virtues of foreign food. Yet you can do a repeat performance in your own kitchen at much less cost, provided VERY fresh fish is available to you from a local market or fishmonger. Oily fish - mackerel, herring and sardines - must be in immaculate condition for success, not frozen, not lying about in packets in the supermarket, not left in the refrigerator for more than a few hours. The emphasis is on fresh.

2 medium to large mackerel
4 sprigs of fresh oregano
2 sprigs of fresh rosemary
4 thinnish slices of fresh, unpeeled but washed ginger

Baste
Juice of ½ lime
1 peeled and crushed clove of garlic
2 tsp olive oil
Sea salt

1 Ask fishmonger to clean mackerel, leaving on heads. Wash each fish inside and out then wipe dry with kitchen paper towels. Make 4 diagonal cuts with a sharp knife on either side of the body so that heat will penetrate better
2 Put 2 sprigs of oregano, 1 of parsley and 2 slices of ginger inside each mackerel then transfer to a foil-lined grill pan.
3 For baste, beat together lime juice, garlic and oil and brush half over the fish. Sprinkle with sea salt and cook under a hot

grill for 5 to 6 minutes or until skin begins to look charred.
4 Turn over, brush with rest of baste and sprinkle with more salt. Grill a further 4 minutes and eat straight away.

Grilled filleted mackerel

Have 2 fresh mackerel filleted (4 fillets). Place flesh sides uppermost, in a grill pan lined with lightly oiled foil. Sprinkle with Worcester sauce, a few drops of malt vinegar and sea salt. Grill 5 minutes without turning.

Grilled sardines or herring

As sardines imported from hot countries are often frozen, small fresh herrings are a preferable option and taste, if anything, less fishy.

Allow 2 to 3 small fish per person. Clean well, leaving on heads. Put into a foil-lined grill pan. Brush with baste given for mackerel or use freshly squeezed lemon juice mixed with pizza oil (flavoured olive oil). Allow 4 teaspoons of oil to every large lemon which will do for about 10 herring. Sprinkle with salt or substitute and grill 3 minutes per side.

Herrings baked with stuffing

SERVES 4

A revival of a recipe I made years ago which lay lost in my personal archives for over twenty years. Eat with jacket potatoes and salad made from grated carrots tossed with a few raisins and appropriate dressing.

4 large fresh herrings, cleaned and with central bones removed
Salt or salt substitute
1 large Cox or Golden Delicious apple
1 smallish onion
1 tbsp chopped (minced) frozen dill
1 tbsp chopped (minced) frozen parsley
75g/3oz/1 ½ cups fresh brown breadcrumbs
2 tsp sunflower oil

1 Set oven to 180C/350F/Gas 4. Lightly oil a fairly shallow heatproof dish or tin.
2 Wash and dry herrings then sprinkle inside and out lightly with salt to taste.
3 Peel apple and onion then grate both fairly finely. Transfer to bowl and mix in dill, parsley and two-thirds of the breadcrumbs.
4 Spoon equal amounts on to insides of herrings then fold each in half over stuffing, head end to tail.
5 Arrange in prepared dish or tin, sprinkle with remaining crumbs then trickle oil over the top of each. Bake for about 35 minutes until well-browned and cooked through.

Tuna in Heaven

SERVES 2 TO 3

A simple mix for a lightish meal. Serve on hot toast or toasted crumpets.

200g/7oz/1 cup can of tuna in olive oil
4 tbsp chopped (minced) dill or watercress leaves
5 spring onions (scallions)
1 tsp prepared mustard, mild or hot depending on taste
2 tbsp thick yogurt
2 tsp tomato purée (paste)
Freshly milled pepper to taste
2 to 3 slices of hot toast or toasted crumpets
Chopped (minced) parsley for garnishing

1 Tip tuna and oil from can into a bowl and fork into flakes.
2 Add dill or watercress.
3 Trim and wash spring onions (scallions) then chop and add to tuna with mustard, yogurt and tomato purée (paste).
4 Season to taste with pepper and spread on toast or crumpets. Sprinkle with parsley and serve.

Fried tuna steak

SERVES 1

If tuna is well and truly fresh and not frozen, it has no smell and should be treated simply and with dignity as it is in places like Madeira, Portugal and South Africa. Now that freshly-caught tuna is flown into Britain on a fairly regular basis, buy a piece for yourself and cook it in this classic style which our local fishmonger recommended. It doesn't need marinating or smothering in sauce when impeccably fresh, a tip worth remembering.

275g/10oz tuna steak
2 tsp olive oil
1 clove of garlic, peeled and crushed
Fresh lemon or lime juice

1 Wash tuna and pat dry with kitchen paper towels.
2 Sizzle oil in a medium frying pan. Mix in garlic and fry gently until light gold.
3 Add fish and fry 9 minutes over a moderate heat, turning twice with 2 spatulas to prevent breaking up the flesh.
4 Lift out on to a warm plate and squeeze over the lemon or lime juice. If liked, garnish with mint or parsley.

Smoked haddock fish cakes with coriander raita

SERVES 4

Old-fashioned and traditional although the Indian raita, flavoured with coriander (cilantro) which is one of today's essential herbs, adds an element of Far Eastern subtlety.

450g/1lb/16oz potatoes
Boiling salted water
225g to 250g/8oz undyed smoked haddock fillet
25g/1oz/$\frac{1}{2}$ cup soft white breadcrumbs
$\frac{1}{2}$ tsp onion salt
$\frac{1}{4}$ tsp lemon grass powder (Schwartz)
1 tbsp chopped (minced) fresh or freeze dried chives
Corinader Raita (see below)

1 To make fish cakes, peel and wash potatoes, cut into chunks and cook in the boiling salted water until tender.
2 Meanwhile, poach haddock in a large shallow frying pan in 2 changes of cold water to reduce salt. Place in pan flesh side down and leave uncovered. Drain and flake up flesh with 2 forks, discarding skin and bones.
3 Drain potatoes and finely mash. Work in fish followed by breadcrumbs and all remaining ingredients. (Except Raita).
4 Leave until cold then shape into 8 balls. Put into a large, non-stick frying pan and flatten each slightly with a fork. Fry 8 minutes, turning once.
5 Transfer to a warm plate and serve with the Raita, which should be made ahead of time.

Coriander Raita
Combine 125g/4oz/$\frac{1}{2}$ cup low fat yogurt with 3 tablespoons chopped (minced) coriander (cilantro) 2 medium blanched,

skinned and chopped tomatoes, $^1/_3$ of a grated unpeeled cucumber, $^1/_4$ tsp turmeric, a peeled and crushed clove of garlic and sugar, salt and pepper to taste.

Macaroni mackerel smoke with nuts

SERVES 4

An easy-going pasta dish which takes just a few minutes to make.

6 large spring onions (scallions)
250g/9oz/about 2 cups quick-cooking macaroni
Boiling salted water
350g/12oz smoked mackerel
4 tbsp shelled pistachios
2 tbsp balsamic vinegar
1 tbsp olive oil
Salt or salt substitute and pepper to taste
4 tbsp chopped (minced) parsley

1 Trim and wash onions (scallions) then coarsely chop. Leave aside for the time being. Cook macaroni in boiling salted water as directed on the packet. Drain and return to pan.
2 While macaroni is cooking, skin mackerel and flake up the flesh.
3 Add to macaroni with the onions, pistachios, vinegar and oil. Toss gently to mix with 2 spoons then adjust seasoning to taste.
5 Spoon on to 4 warm plates and sprinkle with parsley. Serve hot with cooked peas or sprouts.

Fish gratin with leek

SERVES 4

Comfort food for cool days with a light texture and taste to remember. Half-fat cheddar cheese and breadcrumbs make the traditional au gratin style topping.

675g/1 ½ lb/24oz floury potatoes
Boiling salted water
450g/1lb/16oz skinned fillet of cod, haddock or salmon
1 medium leek
1 tbsp sunflower oil
150ml/¼ pt/⅝ cup hot skimmed milk
175g/6oz Philadelphia light cheese with chives
5 tbsp soft brown breadcrumbs
Salt and pepper to taste

<u>Topping</u>
4 tbsp crisp breadcrumbs
4 heaped tbsp grated half fat Cheddar cheese

1 Peel and wash potatoes then cut into chunks. Cook in boiling salted water until tender. Drain and finely mash in the saucepan.
2 Meanwhile poach fish in a little salted water (starting from cold) for 5 to 7 minutes until it looks cooked through and has completely lost its opaque look. Drain and flake. Leave aside for the moment.
3 Trim leek, leaving on 5cm/2 inches of green 'skirt'. Slit lengthwise and wash thoroughly in between leaves to remove mud and grit. Shake dry and cut into thin slices. Put into a saucepan with oil and fry gently until light gold.
4 Set oven to 220C/425F/Gas 7. Stand pan of potatoes over a low heat then beat in milk followed by gradual amounts of cheese.

5 When smooth and fluffy, stir in flaked fish, fried leek and the brown crumbs. Season to taste. Spread mixture into a lightly oiled pie dish, about $1\frac{1}{4}$ litre/2 pint capacity.

6 Sprinkle with topping ingredients then reheat and brown in the oven for about 12 minutes until golden brown and crusty. Serve with a beetroot and onion salad.

Grilled mackerel with tandoori baste

SERVES 4

Fish with zip. Eat with Naan bread and a mixed salad.

4 tbsp apple juice
1 tbsp olive oil
1 tbsp wine vinegar
1 tlsp Tandoori paste
2 dashes of Tabasco
1 tsp salt or substitute
1 tsp tubed or bottled tomato purée (paste)
4 large mackerel, cleaned but with heads left on
1 medium lemon, cut into quarters

1 Beat apple juice with all remaining ingredients except last two.
2 Wash and dry mackerel then make 3 diagonal cuts on each side of body with a sharp knife.
3 Place in a lightly oiled grill pan and brush thickly with baste.
4 Grill 5 minutes, turn over and brush with more baste. Continue to grill a further 4 to 5 minutes.
5 Serve each fish with a wedge of lemon for squeezing over the top.

Tuna fish pie with crackle topping

Serves 4 to 6

A family dish for weekends.

6 medium to large potatoes
1 large onion
Boiling water
Salt or substitute to taste
3 tbsp skimmed milk powder
2 cans (each 7oz/200g/1 cup) tuna in olive oil
Salt or substitute and pepper to taste
6 tbsp toasted breadcrumbs
3 tbsp half fat cheese, grated

1 Peel and wash potatoes then cut into chunks. Peel and quarter onion. Put both into a fairly large saucepan with water and salt.
2 Bring to boil, lower heat and two-thirds cover. Simmer until soft. Drain off water, leaving about 3 tablespoons behind in pan.
3 Mash potatoes and onion in the pan with milk powder, beating until light and fluffy. Set oven to 220C/425F/Gas 7.
4 Mash tuna coarsely with its oil and stir into the mashed potato mixture, seasoning with salt and pepper. Spread evenly into a lightly oiled 23cm/9 inch round heatproof dish.
5 Sprinkle top with crumbs and cheese then heat through and crispen in the oven for about 20 minutes. Eat with lightly cooked cabbage or green beans.

Great canton fish

SERVES 6

To the Chinese, there's no classier fish than sea bass and their delicate technique of cooking it is classic and aesthetic. At twice the price of salmon, bass could be deemed an indulgence but as part of a Chinese meal, one fish will yield about six servings which makes it economically viable. Cooking fish in the microwave equates to Chinese steaming but it 's much less bother and works brilliantly.

1 sea bass weighing about 600g/1 $\frac{1}{4}$ lb/20oz, cleaned but with head left on
$\frac{1}{2}$ tsp caster (superfine) sugar
$\frac{1}{2}$ tsp salt or substitute
1 shallot or 6 spring onions (scallions)
2.5 cm/1 inch piece fresh ginger
5 or 6 sprays of fresh coriander (cilantro)
2 tbsp soy sauce
2 tsp sunflower oil

1 Wash fish inside and out and wipe dry with paper towels.
2 Using a sharp knife, make 3 diagonal slits on either side of the body then season by sprinkling with sugar and salt.
3 Peel shallot (you should find 2 bulbs under the skin) or trim spring onions (scallions). Put into a bowl. Slice ginger and squeeze through a garlic press directly on top.
4 Spread into body cavity of fish then add the coriander (cilantro).
5 Transfer to a dish and trickle the soy sauce and oil over the top. Cover with a matching lid or cling film, slitting twice to allow steam to escape. Cook for 10 minutes at defrost setting in a 650 watt microwave. Stand 2 minutes before serving.

Red sea bream with thai stuffing

SERVES 4

A dazzler. Serve with mixed Oriental pickles, chinese noodles tossed with a trace of sesame oil and jasmine tea or rice wine.

1 red sea bream weighing just over 1kg /2lb/32oz, scaled and gutted but
      with head left on
100g/3 ½ oz shallots
1 bulb of lemon grass (a spring onion or scallion look-alike but with less green)
1 small red chilli
60g/just over 2oz/1 ⅛ cup soft breadcrumbs
2 tsp sesame oil
1 tbsp soy sauce
4 sprigs fresh coriander (cilantro)

1 Wash fish inside and out and pat dry with paper towels. Transfer to a large piece of lightly oiled foil. Set oven to 200° C/400° F/ Gas 6.
2 For stuffing, peel shallots and finely chop (mince) or grate. Peel lemon grass and finely chop (mince). Do the same with the halved and de-seeded chilli, washing your hands immediately afterwards to prevent skin burns.
3 Mix together the shallots, lemon grass, chilli and breadcrumbs then stir in oil and soy sauce. Pack into body cavity of fish then wrap securely in the foil, making a tight parcel.
4 Put into a roasting tin and bake for 50 minutes.
5 Unwrap and remove skin then ease portions of fish away from central bone with 2 spoons and put on to 4 warm plates. Garnish with coriander (cilantro). Accompany with rice, miniature sweet corn and Oriental pickles.

Tip:
Any other red fish may be used from the jack or snapper family.

Moules Marinière

SERVES 3 TO 4

The national dish, institution even, of Belgium where the traditional accompaniment is a mound of frites. Northern France too. In other parts of the world, healthier crusty bread is served instead to mop up the juices. When choosing mussels, make sure the shells are intact and have no cracks. They should be tightly closed or close up quickly when tapped. Mussels are known for their beards. Pull off or cut off with kitchen scissors before cooking then rinse and scrub clean under cold running water. If any mussels stay closed after cooking, throw them away as they will be poisonous and unfit to eat.

3 tbsp olive oil
6 small onions or shallots, peeled and chopped (minced)
1 clove of garlic, peeled and crushed
150ml/$^1\!/_4$ pt/$^5\!/_8$ cup dry white wine
1 bay leaf
2 litres/4pt/10 cups fresh mussels (4lb)
3 tbsp soft breadcrumbs
3 tbsp chopped (minced) parsley

1 Heat oil until sizzling in a large saucepan. Add the onions or shallots and garlic and fry gently for 4 to 5 minutes until the palest gold, stirring frequently.
2 Pour in wine and bay leaf. Bring to the boil, lower heat and simmer slowly for 7 minutes.
3 Stir in mussels, bring liquid back to the boil then reduce heat and cover pan. Steam 5 to 6 minutes until mussels have opened, discarding any that remain closed.
4 Stir in breadcrumbs. Spoon into 4 large soup plates and sprinkle each portion with parsley. Eat straight away.

Note:
Mussels are now being farmed around the West coast of Scotland and the Northern Isles.

♥

Mussels tagliarini

SERVES 2 TO 3

Back to the Med with these mussels in a wine and tomato sauce flavoured with parsley and thyme.

1 $\frac{1}{2}$ litres/3pt/7 $\frac{1}{2}$ to 8 cups fresh mussels (3lb), washed, scrubbed and bearded (see Moules Marinière on page 112)
150ml/ $\frac{1}{4}$ pt/ $\frac{5}{8}$ cup dry white wine
2 tbsp olive oil
2 cloves of garlic, peeled and crushed
1 small onion, peeled and chopped (minced)
Pinch of cayenne pepper
175g/6oz tagliarini or spaghetti, freshly cooked
2 blanched and skinned tomatoes, de-seeded and chopped
Salt and pepper to taste
1 tbsp EACH chopped (minced) fresh parsley and fresh thyme

1 Place mussels in a large pan. Add wine then bring to the boil, lower heat and cover. Steam 5 to 6 minutes until mussels have opened, discarding any that remain closed. Stir once or twice.
2 While mussels are steaming, heat olive oil in a pan. Add the garlic, onion and cayenne pepper. Cook for 1 minute.
3 Put well-drained pasta into a large warm dish. Top with mussels, lifted out of pan with a draining spoon. Keep hot.
4 Strain mussel liquid into the oil and garlic mixture. Boil rapidly until reduced by half then mix in rest of ingredients. Pour over mussels and pasta. Eat straight away.

<u>Note</u>
Adapted from a recipe supplied by the Sea Food Industry Authority of Edinburgh.

Paella

SERVES 4

With a glass or two of Sangria and a sudden charge of sunlight, you could be anywhere on one of Spain's familiar Costas where Paella eating is a national pastime. This one is fairly true to life but demands saffron and a selection of seafood.

4 medium joints of roasting chicken (broilers)
1 large onion
2 cloves of garlic
2 tbsp olive oil
225g/8oz/1¼ cups round grain rice (a good choice is Italian risotto rice)
½ tsp saffron strands, soaked for 20 minutes in 4 tbsp hot water
575ml/1pt/2¼ cups vegetable stock
1 bay leaf
175g/6oz/about 1¼ cups frozen peas
125g/4oz/¾ cup cooked peeled prawns (shrimp)
100g/3½ oz/½ to ¾ cup flaked crabmeat
8 cooked mussels (bottled ones are fine to use)
1 canned or bottled red pepper (pimiento), drained and cut into strips

1 Skin chicken then wash and dry with paper towels. Leave aside temporarily.
2 Peel onion and garlic and chop (mince) both fairly finely. Put into a large saucepan with oil and fry gently until light gold. Add rice and stir fry for 1 minute.
3 Mix in saffron with the water in which it was soaking, the vegetable stock and bay leaf. Bring to the boil, lower heat and simmer for 12 minutes. Spoon into a large heatproof dish, about 8cm/3 inches in depth. Preheat oven to 180C/350F/ Gas 4.
4 Arrange chicken joints on top of rice , cover dish with a lid or foil and oven-cook for 30 minutes. Uncover and continue to cook for a further 15 minutes.

♥

5 Remove from oven and arrange remaining ingredients attractively on top. Leave uncovered and reheat in the oven for about 5 to 7 minutes.

Somerset mussels

SERVES 4

England's answer to Moules Marinière and made with cider, local to Somerset and Hereford.

2 litres/4pt/10 cups fresh mussels (4lb)
1 tbsp sunflower oil
1 medium onion, peeled and chopped
275ml/$\frac{1}{2}$ pt/1 $\frac{1}{4}$ cups dry cider (alcoholic apple juice)
1 bayleaf
Salt and pepper to taste
1 tbsp chopped (minced) parsley

1 Wash, scrub and beard oysters. (Moules Marinière, page 112).
2 Sizzle oil in a large frying pan. Add onion and cook gently until soft and transparent. Pour in cider. Add bay leaf and seasoning. Bring to the boil.
3 Stir in mussels, lower heat and cover. Steam for 5 to 6 minutes until mussels have opened, discarding any which remain closed. Stir once or twice.
4 Transfer mussels to 4 large soup plates, reserving cider liquid. Pour into a pan and boil rapidly until reduced by half. Stir in parsley, pour over mussels and serve with pieces of crusty bread.

Note
Adapted from a recipe supplied by the Sea Fish Industry Authority of Edinburgh.

Russian dill blinis with fish

SERVES 2

Based on beige-coloured buckwheat flour (available from health food shops), the blinis here are a short-cut version of Russia's traditional yeasted pancakes. They are usually accompanied by pickled or smoked fish - cut up rollmops or smoked salmon- and salady things like diced beetroot and chopped onion dressed with lemon juice. Also thick soured cream for which I have substituted thick yogurt to be on the safe side. Another appetising side dish is the Salmon and Sour Cucumber Dressing below.

<u>Blinis</u>
50g/2oz/$\frac{1}{2}$ cup self raising flour
25g/1oz/$\frac{1}{4}$ cup buckwheat flour
25g/1oz/stoneground wholemeal plain flour
1 tsp salt or substitute
1 large egg, broken into a cup
225ml/8 fluid oz/1 cup skimmed milk
3 tbsp chopped (minced) fresh or frozen dill

1 Sift self raising flour into a mixing bowl. Toss in buckwheat and wholemeal flours with salt.
2 Add egg then gradually beat in the milk. Continue to beat until batter is absolutely smooth and there is no obvious sign of lumps.
3 Cover and leave to stand in the cool for 20 minutes. Stir in dill.
4 To cook, heat a smallish and reliable non-stick pan, with a heavy base, until hot.
5 Pour in a tablespoon and a bit of batter and spread out with the back of a spoon to a 13cm/5 inch round. Cook until the underside is golden brown, reducing heat a little under pan if pancakes seem to be darkening too much.

6 Turn over and cook second side until speckly, allowing about 40 seconds. Repeat, using all the batter mixture. Slip Blinis between folds of a clean tea towel to keep warm as they are cooked then serve as suggested. This quantity of batter mix should make 8 Blinis.

Salmon and sour cucumber dressing

Tip 150g/5oz/$^5/_8$ cup thick yogurt into a bowl. Add 125g/4oz/about $^3/_4$ cup smoked salmon, cut into strips, the same amount of chopped (minced) pickled cucumber and 6 chopped (minced) trimmed spring onions (scallions). Season with pepper to taste.

Red salmon 'rösti'

SERVES 4

Given unlimited supplies of ingredients and reasonable cooking facilities, this is the one recipe I would take with me to my desert island in the sun and eat it with curious, unheard of vegetables and dream of snow-clad Alpine peaks. Here is a true treasure, based on Swiss potato rösti. It is like a thick, golden brown and crusty pancake flavoured with dill.

450g to 500g/1lb/16oz floury potatoes
1 can(212g/7oz/1 cup) red salmon
60g/just over 2oz/1 $\frac{1}{8}$ cup soft breadcrumbs
1 small onion
4 rounded tbsp finely chopped (minced) dill
1 tsp grapeseed oil
Freshly-milled pepper to taste

1 Peel, wash and cut potatoes into chunks then cook in boiling salted water until tender. Whatever you do, catch them before they fall to pieces. Drain and finely mash.
2 Tip salmon into bowl and remove black bits of skin and soft bones if you want to, though they are rich in protein and disappear when cooked.
3 Fork into potatoes with breadcrumbs.
4 Peel onion and grate. Add to salmon and potato mixture with dill, oil and pepper to taste.
5 Heat a large, non-stick and heavy-based frying pan (base about 20cm/8-inches) until hot then spread smoothly with all the salmon mixture. Pre-heat grill.
6 Fry Rösti, undisturbed, for about 4 minutes until the underneath is golden and crusty.
7 Transfer to the grill (handle <u>outside</u> which you should be holding) and cook 5 to 6 minutes to brown the top.
8 Cut into 4 portions and serve hot with a salad of mixed green leaves tossed with low fat dressing.

Salmon stroganov

SERVES 4

Top chefs in Britain seemed to have dropped high-speed Stroganov from their repetoire - too antique, perhaps, for today's taste - yet it remains one of the all-time greats, said to have been created over a century ago by the chef of Russian aristocrat and gastronome, Count Paul Stroganov. Originally made with beef, I have used fresh salmon instead and lightened the load still further by substituting yogurt for the more customary thick cream. The epicurian result speaks for itself.

450 to 500g/1lb/16oz skinned salmon fillet
2 tbsp dried onions
3 tbsp boiling water
2 tsp sunflower oil
125g/4oz/about 1 cup coarsely chopped (minced) pickled cucumber
4 tbsp medium sherry
1 $\frac{1}{2}$ tbsp tomato purée (paste)
150g/5oz/$\frac{5}{8}$ cup Greek yogurt (light)
3 tbsp chopped (minced) parsley
Salt or substitute to taste

1 Wash and dry salmon then cut into narrow strips with a sharp knife. Leave aside for the moment.
2 Soak onions in water for about 15 minutes to soften. Drain thoroughly. Fry in a fairly large frying pan, in the oil, for 2 minutes. Stir constantly.
3 Stir in cucumber, sherry and tomato purée (paste). Add salmon and gently stir-fry for about 3 minutes until just cooked.
4 Mix in yogurt, parsley and salt. Reheat briefly before serving with freshly cooked rice and a mixed salad.

Fresh salmon terrine

SERVES 8

Summery. Perfect for a hot weather buffet. Prettily coloured light apricot and garnished with a delicate contrast of sliced fresh limes and cucumber. A smart number for formalish entertaining. Use wild salmon for a rugged texture, farmed for a softer one.

675g to 700g/1 $\frac{1}{2}$ lb/24oz salmon fillet, skinned
1 medium onion
125g/4oz/2 cups soft white breadcrumbs
1 tsp salt or substitute
3 whites from large eggs
Scant $\frac{1}{4}$ tsp allspice
1 medium cucumber
2 limes
Sprays of fresh marjoram for garnishing

1 Brush a 1 $\frac{1}{2}$ litre /2 $\frac{1}{2}$ pt/6 $\frac{1}{4}$ cup glass or pottery loaf pan with sunflower oil. Set oven to 180C/350F/Gas 4.
2 Wash salmon and pat dry with paper towels. Cut into cubes. Peel onion and cut into eighths.
3 Put both into a food processor with crumbs, salt, egg whites and allspice.
4 Pulse to a purée - NOT too fine. Spread into prepared pan and smooth top evenly with a dampened knife.
5 Cover with lightly oiled foil and bake for 1 hour until terrine is firm to the touch and has risen slightly. Cool down, re-cover and refrigerate overnight.
6 Before serving, wash unpeeled cucumber and wipe dry. Cut into hair-thin slices and leave to stand in a bowl for 1 $\frac{1}{2}$ hours so that surplus water drains out. Stir 2 or 3 times. Spin dry in a salad shaker.

7 Wash and dry limes and cut into thin slices. Remove pips. Turn terrine out on to an oblong dish and edge with about three-quarters of the cucumber. Garnish top to taste with rest of cucumber, sliced limes and the marjoram. Cut into slices to serve.

POULTRY, MEAT AND EGGS

White omelet from the Beverly Hills Hotel

SERVES 1

When Kerman Beriker, the general manager of one of California's most prestigious and legendary hotels, The Beverly Hills on Sunset Boulevard, suggested I include this ingenious creation of his in the book, I thought that's luck for you alright, star-studded food with no strings or cholesterol attached. It's an omelet based only on egg-whites and filled with lightly cooked mixed vegetables, the merest dusting of grated parmesan cheese over the top when it's turned out for extra flavour if you think it needs it. Freshly cooked asparagus spears make a stylish filling, as do cut up and warmed artichoke hearts, but you can go even more off-beat woth this easy stir-fry. In 2 teaspoons of sunflower oil in a wok or frying pan, add some sliced water chestnuts, a tablespoon or so of slim and lightly cooked French beans, the same of raisins, 2 teaspoons of broken walnuts and some shredded raw spinach. According to Mr Beriker, anything goes.

3 whites from large eggs
Pinch of salt or substitute
2 heaped tablespoons freshly cooked and piping hot vegetables
1 tsp finely grated Parmesan cheese (optional)

1 Beat eggs and salt together until foamy and pour into a preheated non-stick omelet pan. The whites must not be stiffly whisked, but broken up.
2 Cook exactly as you would an omelet, spreading the puffs of egg white to edges of pan with a spatula. Cook over medium heat until the underneath is golden, fill with vegetables and fold in half in the pan.
3 Carefully slip on to a plate and sprinkle with cheese if using. Eat hot.

Pot chicken with mixed vegetables

SERVES 5 TO 6

A family dish with built-in root vegetables. The only extras you'll need are rice or pasta and something green like sprouts or cabbage.

2 medium onions
1 small turnip
350g/12oz swede (rutabaga)
6 small parsnips
4 medium carrots
3 medium celery stalks
4 shallots
2 tbsp sunflower oil
1 to 1$\frac{1}{2}$ kg/3lb skinned chicken pieces (broilers)
1 vegetable stock cube
275ml/$\frac{1}{2}$ pt/1$\frac{1}{4}$ cups hot water
1 to 1$\frac{1}{2}$ tsp salt or substitute
4 heaped tbsp chopped (minced) parsley

1 Peel onions and thinly slice. Peel turnip and swede and cut into small chunks. Top and tail parsnips and carrots then peel. Wash celery thoroughly and cut into 25cm/1 inch pieces. Peel shallots.
2 Heat oil in a large and heavy-based saucepan. Add onions and mix round in the oil. Cover and fry gently for 10 minutes. Mix in balance of prepared vegetables.
3 Add chicken pieces and stir round gently with vegetables.
4 Crumble stock cube into water and add salt. Pour into pan over vegetables and chicken. Bring to boil, lower heat and cover. Simmer 35 to 40 minutes until chicken is cooked through and vegetables are tender.
5 Spoon into a large warm serving dish, sprinkle thickly with parsley and serve piping hot.

Elizabethan chicken with honey cider baste

SERVES ABOUT 8

During the reign of Elizabeth 1, foods were well-seasoned, sometimes sweet-sour and very highly-spiced to counteract the pungent odours found in cities and towns where hygiene was virtually unknown. Times have changed but chicken with a touch of streetwise nostalgia still warms the hearts and minds of appreciative diners and fills the kitchen with the evocative and festive fragrance of clementines and cloves. Think winter.

1 $^3/_4$ kg/about 3 $^1/_2$ lb roasting chicken (broiler)

3 clementines

6 cloves

3 peeled cloves of garlic

275ml/$^1/_2$ pt/1 $^1/_4$ cups sweet cider (alcoholic apple juice)

2 tbsp clear honey

1 tbsp Japanese Teriyaki sauce

1 vegetable stock cube

2 tbsp cornflour (cornstarch)

2 tbsp cold water

1 tbsp balsamic vinegar

Florets of fresh broccoli, freshly cooked

1 Skin chicken, cuttting away every piece of visible and accesssible fat. Leave the wings because the fat clings to them tenaciously and removing it is not worth the effort.

2 Rinse bird inside and out and wipe dry with paper towels, NOT A CLOTH as it spreads bacteria. Preheat oven to 180C/350F/Gas 4.

3 Wash and dry clementines and press 2 cloves into each. Put inside body of chicken with the garlic. Stand on a grid in a roasting tin.

4 For baste, combine cider with the honey and Teriyaki sauce.

Crumble in stock cube finely. Note liquid will turn cloudy. Stir well to mix then spoon over chicken. Roast for 1 hour 20 minutes, basting every 15 minutes.

5 Take chicken out of the oven. Remove and discard clementines and garlic then transfer bird to a carving board. Keep warm.

6 To make sauce, mix cornflour (cornstarch) smoothly with water. Pour into a saucepan, carefully strain in what's left of the baste then cook, stirring, until sauce comes to the boil and thickens.

7 Simmer 2 minutes, stir in vinegar and serve separately with the chicken, garnished with a fringe of broccoli. Carve chicken as usual.

White stew of chicken with shallots and tarragon

SERVES 6

A French approach to chicken, home cooking at its best.

1 ½ kg/3lb skinned chicken joints (broilers)
425ml/¾ pt/2 cups skimmed milk
2 tsp salt or substitute
4 tsp prepared grainy mustard
125g/4oz shallots
1 can (about 300g/11oz/1 ½ cups) button mushrooms, drained, liquid
    reserved
3 tbsp cornflour (cornstarch)
150ml/¼ pt/⅝ cup reserved mushroom liquid
6 tbsp cold water
1 ½ tsp dried tarragon
100g/3 ½ oz/about ½ cup Greek yogurt (light)
Chopped (minced) parsley

1　Wash chicken and wipe dry with paper towels.
2　Put into a fairly roomy saucepan wih milk, salt and mustard. Bring to boil, lower heat and cover.
3　Peel shallots and add to pan with mushrooms. Re-cover and continue to simmer 30 to 40 minutes until chicken is tender.
4　Lift pieces out on to a plate and leave aside for the moment.
5　Mix cornflour (cornstarch) smoothly with mushroom liquid and water. Stir into pan juices with tarragon. Bring to the boil, stirring continuously. Simmer 1 to 2 minutes until sauce has thickened.
6　Gradually whisk in yogurt then replace chicken. Reheat without boiling until hot.
7　Transfer chicken and mushroom sauce to hot plates and sprinkle each portion thickly with parsley. Eat with baby boiled potatoes and mange tout.

Seared chicken with green pepper-corns and paprika

SERVES 4

With a squeeze of lemon and a leafy salad, this is a sound investment for health and heart. Eat with jacket potatoes, split open and packed with yogurt, chopped spring onions and seasoning to taste. Allow 4 hours marinating time.

8 large and fleshy chicken thighs (broilers)
2 tsp shop-bought bottled green peppercorn purée (paste)
1 tsp bottled or tubed garlic paste
2 tsp lemon juice
3 tsp tubed vegetable purée (paste)
1 tsp paprika (sweet paprika)
3 tbsp thick yogurt

1 Skin thighs. Well-wash and wipe dry with paper towels. Arrange in a glass dish in a single layer, flesh sides uppermost.
2 Combine rest of ingredients well together to make marinade. Spread half over chicken. Turn thighs over and spread undersides with rest of marinade.
3 Cover and marinate for 2 hours in the cool. Turn over and continue to marinate for a further 2 hours.
4 To cook, arrange chicken in a roasting tin, flesh sides up. Grill for 20 to 25 minutes until meat looks charred and is thoroughly done.

Chicken poivrade

SERVES 4

A cousin of Pepper Steak in a well-heeled sauce flavoured with green Madagascan peppercorns, freshly-milled black pepper and anchovy. An amiable side-kick would be mashed potatoes or pasta with freshly-cooked French beans (sometimes called Kenya beans as they now come from there) tossed with no more than one teaspoon of unsalted butter.

4 large chicken portions (broilers)
1 vegetable stock cube
8 tbsp water
2 tbsp tubed vegetable purée (paste)
3 tbsp green peppercorns in brine, drained
1 ½ tbsp cornflour (cornstarch)
3 tbsp cold water
½ tsp anchovy paste
¼ tsp freshly-milled black pepper
100g/3 ½ oz/½ cup low fat fromage frais or quark
2 tsp Worcester sauce

1 Skin chicken. Wash well and dry with paper towels. Put into a large and fairly deep frying pan, flesh side facing (uppermost).
2 Crumble stock cube into water then stir in vegetable purée (paste). Pour over chicken in pan then sprinkle with peppercorns.
3 Bring to the boil, lower heat and cover. Simmer 15 minutes. Carefully turn each piece of chicken over, bring back to the boil, lower heat and cover. Simmer 45 minutes.
4 To complete, blend cornflour (cornstarch) smoothly with cold water then stir in anchovy paste and pepper. Lift chicken out of pan into a large warm dish.
5 Pour cornflour (cornstarch) liquid into pan juices and bring to the boil, stirring continuously.
6 Simmer 2 minutes, gradually blending in fromage frais and Worcester sauce. Pour over chicken.

Hot and spicy legs

SERVES 4

Most times it's wings that are given the hot and spicy treatment but it works just as well with legs and does much to brighten up their predictable personality. Eat with Chinese noodles and finely-shredded and lightly-cooked dark green cabbage.

8 plump chicken legs (broilers)
200ml/7 fluid oz/⅞ cup pineapple juice
1 tsp chilli and garlic sauce, shop bought in bottles
1 tbsp red wine vinegar
1 tbsp Worcester sauce
1 tbsp tomato ketchup
1 tbsp soy sauce
1 tbsp cornflour (cornstarch)
2 tbsp water

1 Skin legs then wash and dry with paper towels. Put into a large and heavy-based frying pan and dry-fry for 15 minutes over a medium heat. Turn 2 or 3 times to ensure browning is even.
2 In bowl or basin, beat pineapple juice with next 5 ingredients
3 Mix cornflour to smooth liquid with water. Add to pineapple mixture then spoon over chicken.
4 Bring to the boil, lower heat and cover. Simmer slowly for 30 minutes, adding a little extra hot water if liquid in pan seems to be evaporating too much - you should be left with only a small amount of thickish, glossy sauce.

Chicken under crust

SERVES 4

A marvellous one if you're in a hurry and want to get a meal on the table in under 30 minutes. It's microwaved for speed and the idea of the bread topping was given to me by old friend and colleague, Peter Ritchie. Eat with spinach pasta and a mixed salad.

4 chicken portions (broilers) each about 225g/8oz
150g/5oz/$^5/_8$ cup Greek yogurt (light)
2 tsp whole grain dry mustard powder
1 tsp paprika (sweet paprika)
$^1/_4$ tsp dried thyme
$^1/_2$ tsp salt or substitute
$^1/_2$ tsp Worcester sauce
1 tbsp tomato purée (paste)
Crisp wholemeal breadcrumbs, bought in a drum or packet

1 Skin chicken then wash and dry with paper towels. Arrange, flesh sides up, in a large round dish suitable for the microwave. Make sure chicken forms a single layer and is not piled up.
2 Stir yogurt with all remaining ingredients except crumbs and spoon evenly over chicken.
3 Sprinkle thickly with crumbs. Cover with plastic wrap, snip twice with kitchen scissors to allow steam to escape and cook 16 minutes at full power.
4 Leave to stand 3 minutes before eating.

Chopstick chicken with bamboo shoots

SERVES 4

An Oriental attraction, quickly-prepared using already-cooked chicken and a selection of fresh and canned vegetables. Eat with Chinese style noodles and little dishes of soy and chilli sauces to spice the whole thing up.

350g/12oz/about 4 cups cold cooked chicken
2 medium or 1 large leek
2 cloves of garlic
225g/8oz cauliflower
2 tbsp sunflower oil
1 can (225g/8oz/1 cup) sliced bamboo shoots in water, drained, liquid
    reserved
1 tbsp light brown muscovado sugar
1 tsp 5-spice powder
1 $\frac{1}{2}$ tblp cornflour (cornstarch)
225ml/8 fluid oz/1 cup cold water
50ml/2 fluid oz/$\frac{1}{4}$ cup reserved bamboo shoot liquid
2 tbsp tomato ketchup
2 tbsp soy sauce
2 tbsp Worcester sauce
$\frac{1}{2}$ tsp salt or substitute

1 Cut chicken into bite-size pieces.
2 Trim leeks, slit lengthwise and rinse under cold running water, removing earth and grit between leaves. Shake dry and fairly thinly slice. Peel garlic and slice. Divide cauliflower into small florets, removing stalks.
3 Heat oil until sizzling in a large frying pan or wok. Add vegetables, including bamboo shoots, and stir-fry 5 minutes.
4 Meanwhile, mix together sugar, 5-spice powder and cornflour (cornstarch). Gradually blend in cold water, bamboo shoot

♥

liquid and all remaining ingredients. Stir until smooth.

5 Add cut-up chicken to vegetables and fry fairly briskly for 2 minutes. Mix in sugar and spice mixture and bring to the boil, stirring. Lower heat, cover and simmer over a low heat for 10 minutes, stirring several times to prevent sticking.

Crackling drumsticks

SERVES 4

Easy-make, high-fibre, branflake-coated chicken drumsticks, baked until crunchy with a hint of curry for Indian food fanciers or 5-spice powder if Chinese is more your scene. Either way, eat with freshly cooked basmati rice and a salad made of sliced tomatoes and wafer-thin shreds of leek, sprinkled with low-fat salad dressing (vinaigrette).

8 large and fleshy chicken drumsticks (broilers)
75g/3oz/about 1 $\frac{1}{2}$ cup branflakes
4 tsp mild Korma curry powder or 2 tsp 5-spice powder
150g/5oz/$\frac{5}{8}$ cup low fat yogurt
1 tsp salt or substitute

1 Set oven to 190C/375F/Gas 5.
2 Skin drumsticks then wash and wipe dry with paper towels.
3 Put branflakes with curry powder or spice powder into a paper bag and crush down with a rolling pin. Tip out on to a piece of foil.
4 Pour yogurt into a deepish plate and stir in salt. Add drumsticks, one at a time, and turn until coated. Toss in the crushed cornflakes, making sure flesh is well-covered and that there are no thin patches.
5 Transfer to a roasting tin lined with lightly oiled foil. Bake for 30 minutes. Switch off heat and leave drumsticks in the oven for a further 10 minutes before eating.

Thai chicken curry

SERVES 4

Facts and figures sent from the producers of coconut milk (Lotus/Amoy) show it to be free of fat and salt, making it a safe bet for a light and mildly-tempered chicken stew with origins in the Far East. Fortunately for Western cooks, the complex and authentic mix of ingredients for the curry paste, vital for success, has been conveniently blended together by a number of manufacturers and is available in jars from delicatessens and some of the larger supermarket chains, particularly in areas with ethnic communities.

1kg/2lb/32oz boned chicken breasts (broilers), skinned
1 can(400ml/16 fluid oz/2 cups) coconut milk
2 tbsp green Thai curry paste
2 tsp Thai fish sauce
Finely grated peel and juice of $\frac{1}{2}$ lime
Salt or substitute to taste
2 tsp cornflour (cornstarch)
2 tbsp cold water

1 Wash and dry chicken then cut flesh into bite-size cubes.
2 Put the coconut milk into saucepan with the curry paste and bring slowly to the boil, stirring continuously.
3 Add chicken, fish sauce and the lime peel with juice. Season with salt, heat until hot and bubbly then lower heat and cover. Simmer slowly for 50 minutes.
4 Blend cornflour (cornstarch) smoothly with water. Stir into curry and continue to stir – cook uncovered until thickened. Serve with brown rice and vegetable pickle.

The big chicken stir fry

SERVES 4

Something for the wok pot with Oriental overtones. Eat with jasmine rice and pickles.

350g/12oz skinned and boned chicken breast (broilers), cut into strips
175g/6oz/2 cups mange tout (snow peas) fresh or frozen
1 large pack frozen stir-fry mix
125g/4oz/2 cups trimmed and sliced mushrooms
1 tbsp sunflower oil
2 to 3 tsp Indonesian stir-fry seasoning mix
1 tbsp cornflour (cornstarch)
4 tbsp EACH water and medium sherry
1 tbsp soy sauce
1 tsp wine vinegar
1 tsp salt or substitute

1 Wash and dry chicken with paper towels. Top and tail mange tout (snow peas) if fresh.
2 Put fresh or frozen peas into a large bowl with the stir-fry mix and mushrooms. Toss well to mix.
3 Heat oil in a large wok. Add chicken and stir-fry 4 minutes. Add prepared vegetables and continue to stir-fry fairly briskly for 5 minutes.
4 Blend seasoning mix and cornflour (cornstarch) smoothly with rest of ingredients.
5 Add to wok and continue to stir-fry until ingredients look glossy and liquid has thickened; about 1 to 2 minutes.

Mexican chicken mole

SERVES 4

Pronounced Molay, this is Central America's answer to chicken stew with its own dark secret - the addition of plain chocolate. No, it isn't revolting at all and the gravy turns a warm deep brown with a slightly fiery/spicy kick-back. Serve it with white rice and red kidney beans.

12 fairly small portions of skinned chicken
3 tbsp plain (all-purpose) flour
2 tbsp sunflower oil
2 medium red onions
275ml/$\frac{1}{2}$ pt/1 $\frac{1}{4}$ cups tomato juice
125ml/$\frac{1}{4}$ pt/$\frac{5}{8}$ cup vegetable stock
$\frac{1}{4}$ tsp tabasco
2 tbsp dried red and green pepper flakes
1 tsp salt or substitute
1 peeled and crushed clove of garlic
$\frac{1}{2}$ tsp allspice
$\frac{1}{2}$ tsp cinnamon
25g/1oz/1 square plain dark chocolate

1 Wash chicken and dry with paper towels. Coat each portion evenly with flour.
2 Heat oil in a heavy-based and fairly large saucepan. Add coated chicken and fry smartly over a briskish heat until golden brown, turning frequently. Beware spluttering !
3 Using kitchen tongs, remove chicken to a dish. Peel and chop onions. Add to pan and fry in remaining oil until pale gold.
4 Stir in all remaining ingredients except chocolate. Bring to boil and replace chicken. Cover and simmer gently for 45 minutes.
5 Break up chocolate and add piece by piece to the pan, stirring until melted.

Chicken tikka masala

SERVES 6

One of Britain's favourite imports, the Tikka Masala is an exquisite example of a fairly mild and gracious curry from the North of India, classically scented with Eastern herbs and spices and cooled with yogurt. It is less difficult to make at home than one would suppose and is traditionally eaten in the West with Indian bread or Basmati rice.

675g to 700g/1 ½ lb/24oz skinned and boned chicken breast (broiler)
2 medium onions, peeled
2 cloves of garlic, peeled
5cm/2 inch piece of fresh ginger, peeled
1 to 2 green chillies
1 tbsp fresh or frozen chopped (minced) mint
1 tbsp lemon juice
1 tbsp peanut (groundnut) oil
2 tsp paprika (sweet paprika)
¼ tsp cayenne pepper (optional)
2 tsp garam masala
¼ tsp grated nutmeg
1 tsp turmeric
2 tbsp tomato purée (paste)
1 tsp salt or substitute
150g/5oz/⅝ cup Greek yogurt (light)
Chopped (minced) fresh or frozen coriander

1 Wash chicken, dry with paper towels then cut into bite-size pieces. Put into a glass or enamel bowl.
2 Cut onions into chunks. Halve garlic. Slice ginger. Slit chillies, remove inside seeds and wash hands at once to prevent skin burns. Grind all 4 ingredients together in a food processor.
3 Add to chicken with mint, lemon juice and oil then stir in all remaining ingredients except yogurt and coriander. Mix thoroughly, cover and marinate in the refrigerator for 6 to 12 hours.

4 To cook, tip ingredients into a heavy-based pan. Bring to boil, stirring, then reduce heat and cover. Simmer 40 minutes, stirring several times.

5 Stir in yogurt and sprinkle each portion with coriander.

Casserole of curried chicken

SERVES 4

An apology for a true curry but the compensations are speed and minimal time involved in preparation. Eat with rice of Indian bread and chutney. Also a salad.

4 boned chicken breasts (broilers)
250g/10oz/1 $\frac{1}{4}$ cups low fat yogurt
1 to 2 tsp mild Korma curry powder
$\frac{1}{2}$ tsp allspice
1 to 2 cloves of garlic, peeled and crushed
$\frac{1}{4}$ tsp cayenne pepper
1 tsp paprika (sweet paprika)
Seeds from 2 opened-out cardamom pods
1 tsp salt or substitute
1 tbsp tomato purée (paste)
Juice of $\frac{1}{2}$ a lime
1 tsp caster sugar

1 Set oven to 190C/375F/Gas 5
2 Skin chicken breasts then wash and wipe dry with paper towels. Put into a suitable casserole dish in a single layer.
3 Tip yogurt into a bowl, add all remaining ingredients and stir thoroughly to mix.
4 Spoon over chicken. Cover dish securely with a matching lid or foil and bake for 1 hour.

Chicken tagine

SERVES 6

A Middle Eastern/North African stew, presently the 'in' thing and quite smart to be seen with in restaurants, the Tagine is gilded with saffron, spiced with cinnamon and feted with abundance of lightly fried onions. Sometimes spelled with a j instead of a g, I've seen it with olives, with prunes, with almonds, even dates but my prime choice is for the one with chick peas and dried apricots (still authentic) with a heady fragrance all its own. Eat with Arab bread or seedy Greek but if you want to keep the Eastern theme going, serve with cous-cous (page 178) lightly spotted with raisins and dusted with a hint of mint and ground cinnamon.

$\frac{1}{2}$ tsp saffron strands
200ml/8 fluid oz/1 cup hot water
450g to 500g/1lb/16oz onions
2 cloves of garlic
2 tbsp olive oil
1 tsp powdered cinnamon
Juice of 1 lemon
1$\frac{1}{2}$ kg/3lb/48oz fleshy chicken (broilers) drumsticks
100g/3$\frac{1}{2}$ oz dried apricots
1 can (400g/14oz/2 cups) chick peas (gabanzos)
40g/1$\frac{1}{2}$ oz/$\frac{1}{2}$ cup flaked almonds, lightly toasted
4 heaped (heaping) tbsp chopped (minced) parsley

1 Soak saffron strands in the water for 30 minutes to draw out colour and flavour.
2 Peel and thinly slice onions. Put into a saucepan then peel garlic and crush over the top through a garlic press. Mix in oil and fry gently, covered, for about 30 to 35 minutes until onions have softened to a creamy-gold mass - a bit like coarse purée.

140

3 Stir in cinnamon and lemon juice. Skin drumsticks, wash and dry with paper towels then add to pan with apricots, chick peas (gabanos) and liquid from can. Stir in almonds

4 Bring slowly to the boil, lower heat and cover. Simmer for 30 to 40 minutes until drumsticks are tender and completely cooked through.

5 Spoon into a serving dish and sprinkle with parsley. Eat straight away, while still very hot.

Char-grill texas chicken

SERVES 4

Tex-Mex at your fingertips. Using a Le Creuset Grillet or Tefal's Fitness Frying Pan, cook chicken breasts in either of these heavy-based, ridged pans for the typical char-grill effect you see in restaurants. Eat with sweetcorn and jacket potatoes.

4 medium skinned and boned chicken breasts (broilers)
8 tsp Texan Pan-Fry seasoning

1 Wash chicken breasts and wipe dry with paper towels. Sprinkle thickly on all sides with the seasoning.

2 Put into the Grillet or Fitness Frying Pan and fry 17 minutes, turning 4 times until both sides are a deep golden brown.

3 Switch off heat and leave chicken to stand for 5 minutes, turning twice before eating.

Jamaican jerk chicken

SERVES 4

Caribbean in character and just right for the barbecue or grill, this recipe comes from Schwartz, the herb and spice people, who make the Jerk seasoning. It's spicy without being overwhelming and is only marginally hot.

1 tsp sunflower oil

2 tsp soy sauce

1 tbsp Jamaican Jerk Seasoning

8 large chicken thighs or legs (broilers) skinned

1 Make a paste with the oil, soy sauce and seasoning,

2 Wash chicken and dry with paper towels. Spread paste over all sides and put into a dish in a single layer.

3 Cover loosely and leave to marinate in the refrigerator for 2 hours.

4 Grill or barbecue for 30 minutes, turning frequently. Eat with other barbecued foods.

Neapolitan chicken

SERVES 4

Another quickie option for busy cooks. Eat with hot macaroni tossed with the merest touch of pesto or dried tomato paste.

4 medium chicken joints (broilers)
1 can (400g/14oz/about 2 cups) tomatoes in tomato juice
1 large green pepper (bell pepper)
1 large onion, peeled
1 level tsp salt or substitute
1 tsp Italian seasoning (dried herb mix)

1 Set oven to 190C/375F/Gas 5. Have ready a fairly large casserole dish with matching lid or piece of lightly oiled foil for covering.
2 Skin chicken then wash and dry with paper towels. Put into casserole in a single layer and coat with tomatoes and liquid from can.
3 Wash, dry and halve pepper then remove inside fibres and seeds. Cut flesh into narrow strips. Thinly slice onion and separate slices into rings. Add both to casserole.
4 Season with salt and sprinkle seasoning over the top. Cover securely and bake for 1 hour.

Turkey cous-cous

SERVES 4 VERY HUNGRY PEOPLE

France was my training ground for Cous-Cous making, a long-established and highly-respected North African import which the French adopted a long time ago and now eat regularly with the same enthusiasm and dedication we reserve over here for Indian food. The combination of a distinctive stew and the semolina cereal which goes with it - namely Cous-Cous - is fairly painstaking to make and is therefore not a daily occurence in French restaurants. It may appear on the menu once, maybe twice, a week, portions gargantuan, the sight and smell appetising beyond belief. Worth waiting for. Usually made with lamb, chicken and spicy sausages called Merguez, I've used lean turkey legs instead and the taste is stupendous. A characterful North African accompaniment/condiment with built-in heat is Harissa, now available from Bart Spices, and part and parcel of the whole Cous-Cous deal though can be by-passed by those who are anti-fire in food.

<u>The stew</u>
4 medium turkey drumsticks, each about 350g/12oz
2 large onions
3 cloves of garlic
3 medium carrots
4 medium courgettes (zucchini)
1 tbsp olive oil
4 large blanched and skinned tomatoes
$\frac{1}{2}$ tsp cinnamon
$\frac{1}{4}$ tsp ground ginger
2 to 2$\frac{1}{2}$ tsp salt or substitute
Between $\frac{1}{4}$ and 1 tsp chilli sauce or Harissa
450ml/$\frac{3}{4}$ pt/1$\frac{1}{2}$ cups hot water
1 can (400g/14oz/2 cups) chick peas (gabanzos)
4 tbsp finely chopped (minced) parsley

1 Skin drumsticks then wash and dry with paper towels. Leave aside for the moment.

2 Peel onions and garlic then slice both thinly, separating onion slices into rings. Peel carrots and thickly slice. Top and tail courgettes (zucchini) and cut like carrots. Rinse prepared vegetables and leave to drain.

3 Heat oil in a large and heavy pan until sizzling. Add onions and garlic. Fry slowly 15 to 20 minutes until they begin to soften, keeping pan two-thirds covered. Add drumsticks, one at a time, and fry until golden on all sides. Lift out on to a plate and cover loosely.

4 Add carrots and courgettes to pan and lightly fry for about 5 minutes, stirring periodicaly.

5 Chop tomatoes and tip into a bowl. Add cinnamon, ginger, salt and chilli sauce or Harissa. Stir into fried vegetables with water. Bring to the boil, replace drumsticks, lower heat and cover. Simmer for 1 hour 20 minutes.

6 Drain chick peas and add to pan with parsley, stirring in gently. Re-cover and continue to simmer slowly for 20 to 30 minutes until drumsticks are tender and cooked through.

7 To serve, mound hot Cous-Cous (page 178) on to centres of 4 large and pre-warmed deepish plates. Place a drumstick on top of each then surround with vegetables and some gravy. Serve remaining gravy separately in a warm dish.

Turkey chop suey

SERVES 4

A North American interpretation of a Chinese stir-fry, closely related to Chow Mein, also Transatlantic. Serve with noodles, pickles and dishes of chilli and soy sauces.

350g/12oz cold cooked turkey
1 medium onion
1 large celery stalk
1 large green pepper (bell pepper)
25 cm/1 inch piece of fresh ginger
225g/8oz bean sprouts
2 tbsp cornflour (cornstarch)
1 tbsp bottled oyster sauce
2 tbsp bottled Hoisin sauce
2 tbsp soy sauce
225ml/8 fluid oz/ 1 cup water
$\frac{1}{2}$ to 1 tsp salt or substitute
1 tbsp sunflower oil

1 Cut turkey into strips.
2 Peel onion and chop. Wash and dry celery then cut into thin slices. Wash, dry and halve pepper then remove inside fibres and seeds. Cut flesh into strips. Peel ginger, cut into small pieces and crush through a garlic press on to a saucer. Rinse bean sprouts and thoroughly drain.
3 To prepare thickener, mix cornflour (cornstarch) smoothly with oyster and Hoisin sauces then stir in water and salt.
4 Sizzle oil in large frying pan or wok. Add all prepared ingredients with ginger and bean sprouts. Stir-fry briskly 4 minutes.
5 Mix in turkey and continue to stir-fry for a further 4 minutes.

Turkey stew with sweetcorn

SERVES 4

An old-fashioned stew for winter warmth. Eat with boiled potatoes and sprouts.

450g to 500g/1lb/16oz turkey breast without bone
450g to 500g/1lb/16oz frozen vegetable stewpack
225g/8oz/1 ½ to 2 cups frozen sweetcorn
425ml/¾ pt/2 cups hot water
1 ½ tsp salt or substitute
25g/1oz/½ cup soft breadcrumbs
1 tsp dried marjoram
3 tbsp chopped (minced) parsley

1 Cut turkey into bite-size pieces and put into a large saucepan with vegetables, water and salt. Bring to boil, lower heat and cover. Simmer 50 minutes to 1 hour until turkey is tender.
2 Stir in breadcrumbs and marjoram. Simmer 5 minutes then transfer to 4 large warm plates. Sprinkle parsley over each serving.

Juniper turkey

SERVES 6

With rosé wine, quince jelly and flavour of gin - plus a shot of it too - this spells cheers.

675g/1 ½ lb/24oz raw turkey meat, breast or leg according to taste
275ml/½ pt/1 ¼ cups rosé wine
4 tbsp gin
2 bay leaves
4 juniper berries
2 cloves of garlic
¼ tsp dried thyme
1 tsp salt or substitute
1 tbsp sunflower oil
1 tbsp plain (all-purpose) flour
8 tbsp cold water
2 tbsp quince jelly

1 Wash turkey and dry with paper towels. Cut into bite-size cubes. Put into a mixing bowl and pour in wine and gin.
2 Break each bay leaf into 2 or 3 pieces. Coarsely crush juniper berries between finger and thumb. Peel and crush garlic. Stir all three into turkey mixture with thyme and salt then cover bowl and marinate in the refrigerator 8 hours.
3 Heat oil in a fairly large and sturdy pan until it starts to sizzle. Add turkey, a few pieces at a time, and fry briskly until flesh loses its raw look and liquid in the pan evaporates.
4 Strain in wine marinade and bring to the boil. Lower heat and cover. Simmer 40 to 45 minutes until tender.
5 To complete, mix flour smoothly with gradual amounts of water. Stir into turkey mixture with quince jelly. Bring back to the boil, stirring continually.

6 Simmer, stirring, for 3 minutes or until gravy has thickened. Serve with brown rice and green vegetables to taste.

Juniper venison

Make as previous recipe, substituting the same amount of diced venison.

Turkey in tomatoes

Serves 4

Designed for brightness and lightness, sunny days, easy living. Eat with freshly cooked polenta (page 176) or pasta shells tossed with a trace of Tapenade (page 60).

4 large beef tomatoes
225g/8oz raw turkey mince
50g/2oz/1 cup soft breadcrumbs
1 clove of garlic, peeled
3 tbsp chopped (minced) parsley
15g/$\frac{1}{2}$ oz/about $\frac{1}{8}$ cup sunflower seeds
$\frac{1}{2}$ to 1 tsp salt or substitute
275ml/$\frac{1}{2}$ pt/1 $\frac{1}{4}$ cups vegetable stock

1 Set oven to 190C/375F/Gas 5.
2 Wash and dry tomatoes and cut centrally in half. Remove insides with a curved grapefruit knife, put on to board and roughly chop. Keep tomato shells, placing them upside down to drain on paper towels.
3 Put chopped tomato pulp into a bowl then fork in turkey mince and crumbs.
4 Crush in garlic then fork in parsley, sunflower seeds and salt. Continue to stir until ingredients are thoroughly combined.
5 Arrange tomato shells in a 8cm/3-inch tall and lightly oiled heatproof dish. Fill with equal amounts of turkey mixture, pour in stock then bake, uncovered, for 30 minutes. Serve hot.

Turkey patties

SERVES 4

Undemanding, unproblematic and economical, the Patties make a wholesome meal when eaten hot with mashed potatoes and baked beans, cold with salad.

1 medium onion
75g/3oz/1 ½ cups soft brown breadcrumbs
450g/1lb/16oz raw turkey mince
3 tbsp water
1 tsp salt or substitute

1 Peel onion and finely grate.
2 Put crumbs into a mixing bowl then add turkey, grated onion, water and salt.
3 Fork ingredients together until evenly-combined then divide into 16 pieces of equal size.
4 Shape into flattish patties and fry without fat, a few at a time, in a non-stick pan. Allow a total of 7 to 8 minutes for each batch and turn once.

Tip:
Chutney or tomato ketchup make companionable accompaniments.

Turkey in the wok with soya vermicelli

SERVES 4

A hint of mystery here brought about by the inclusion of one of the most unlikely ingredients you could think of - lemon marmalade. Funny ? Make it and you'll soon discover how it lifts and beautifies the taste of this vaguely Chinese stir-fry.

1 tbsp cornflour (cornstarch)
6 tbsp cold water
$\frac{1}{2}$ tsp Worcester sauce
2 tsp soy sauce
2 tbsp lemon marmalade
450g/1lb/16oz raw turkey mince
350g/12oz/about 2 cups Chinese stir-fry vegetable mix

<u>To serve</u>
About 200g/7oz soya vermicelli (slightly opaque, fine and white), cooked as directed on the packet

1 Make thickener first. Mix cornflour (cornstarch) with cold water then stir in Worcester and soy sauces and marmalade.
2 Put turkey into a non-stick wok and stir-fry fairly briskly for 6 minutes. Add vegetable mix and stir-fry briskly for a further 3 minutes.
3 Stir in cornflour (cornstarch) liquid and cook until mixture comes to the boil and thickens. Fork in vermicelli and briefly reheat.

Turkey loaf with red wine sauce

SERVES 4 TO 6

A microwave item which is perfectly-mannered and a fine example of fast food. The sauce round it comprises only four ingredients yet has a sturdy and full flavour, delicious - and a bit Scandinavian - with mashed potatoes and cranberry sauce.

450g/1lb/16oz raw turkey mince
1 vegetable stock cube
Finely grated peel of $^1/_2$ medium lemon
$^1/_4$ tsp Italian seasoning (dried herbs)
$^1/_2$ tsp salt or substitute
50g/2oz/1cup soft brown breadcrumbs
6 tbsp cold water

Sauce
150ml/$^1/_4$ pt/$^5/_8$ cup red wine
2 tbsp vegetable purée (paste)
1 tsp soft dark brown sugar
$^1/_4$ tsp salt

1 Put turkey into a bowl and crumble in stock cube.
2 Add all remaining ingredients then work loaf together with your hands until evenly-combined. Shape into a rectangle measuring 15cm by 8 cm (6 inches by 3 inches).
3 Transfer to a glass or pottery microwave dish and, with knife, score a criss-cross pattern on top.
4 For sauce, beat wine smoothly with rest of ingredients listed then spoon over loaf.
5 Cover with cling film, slitting it once or twice to allow steam to escape.
6 Cook at defrost setting in a 650 watt microwave for 30 minutes. Stand 5 minutes then slice and serve with sauce.

Turkey tikka

SERVES 4

Charred under a red hot grill, you'd be hard pressed to find fault with this Indian speciality which looks as though it had been cooked in a tandoor or clay oven. Serve splashed with lemon juice and eat with the usual Tandoori accompaniments - Indian bread and a salad of shredded lettuce and cut-up tomatoes.

150g/5oz/⅝ cup low fat yogurt
3 tbsp bright orange Tandoori paste
4 tbsp chopped (minced) fresh coriander
450g to 500g/1lb/16oz turkey breast, weighed without skin and bone

1 Combine yogurt and tandoori paste in a fairly shallow dish or bowl. Stir in coriander.
2 Wash turkey and dry with paper towels. Cut into bite-size cubes, add to yogurt mixture and stir round and round until every piece is thoroughly coated.
3 Cover securely and leave to marinate in the refrigerator for 12 hours.
4 To cook, arrange turkey in a foil-lined grill pan.
5 Stand under a preheated hot grill and grill 5 minutes. Turn over and continue to grill for a further 5 minutes when turkey will take on a slightly charred appearance - exactly as it should look. Eat straight away.

Dutch turkey hash

SERVES 6

Influenced by the cuisine of Indonesia, THE ethnic food of The Netherlands, nothing succeeds better in making a meal of left-over turkey than this interestingly-flavoured hash. With Oriental noodles, some hot sauces and mixed vegetable pickle, you can capture a far-away atmosphere with the least possible effort and feed six people generously without spending a fortune.

5 tbsp dried onion flakes
1 tbsp sunflower oil
3 tbsp plain (all-purpose) flour
425ml/^{3}⁄$_4$ pt/2 cups vegetable stock, warm but not hot
2 bay leaves
1 blade mace or ^{1}⁄$_4$ tsp grated nutmeg
4 tbsp malt vinegar
2 tbsp soy sauce
1 tbsp brown sugar
Salt or substitute and pepper to taste
^{1}⁄$_4$ tsp chilli sauce
450g to 500g/1lb/16oz cold cooked turkey

1 Put onion flakes and oil into a large saucepan. Fry about 2 to 3 minutes over a very low heat until onions are golden brown but not burnt.
2 Stir in flour then gradually blend in stock. Bring to boil, stirring continuously.
3 Simmer gently 5 minutes. Stir in all remaining ingredients, cover pan and bubble gently for 30 minutes.

Venison with chestnuts and whisky

SERVES 4

Venison is affordable for the good times, festivals, celebrations, the healthiest meat you can eat, virtually nil cholesterol, essentially stylish and succulent when braised or stewed as the Scots will vouch for. Townies can readily find it in some of the larger supermarket chains, country folk from local farms and family butchers, and it's a perfect winter meat to eat with confidence by anyone told to cut down on fat.

450g to 500g/1lb/16oz diced venison
225g/8oz/about 2 cups frozen casserole mix (carrots, turnips, swede or
      rutabaga, carrots and celery)
1 can condensed consommé (Campbell's)
$\frac{1}{2}$ tsp Sichuan pepper
1 tbsp redcurrant jelly
1 $\frac{1}{2}$ tbsp orange marmalade
1 tbsp Balsamic vinegar
1 unpeeled satsuma, washed and sliced
1 bay leaf
Half a can (240g/8oz to 9oz/about 1 $\frac{1}{2}$ cups) whole peeled chestnuts, drained
1 tbsp cornflour (cornstarch)
3 tbsp cold water
2 tbsp whisky

1 Wash and dry venison with paper towels. Put into a sturdy non-stick pan and dry-fry over medium heat until all the liquid has evaporated and meat begins to brown. Stir frequently.
2 Add vegetables. Continue to fry until liquid has again evaporated. Allow plenty of time rather than a high heat which can cause burning.
3 Stir in undiluted consommé, Sichuan pepper, redcurrant jelly, marmalade, vinegar, satsuma, bay leaf and chestnuts.
4 Bring to the boil, lower heat and cover. Simmer gently about 1 to 1 $\frac{1}{4}$ hours until meat is soft and tender, allowing a

♥

little extra time if necessary.

5 To complete, blend cornflour (cornstarch) smoothly with water. Add to meat and cook until mixture boils and bubbles, stirring all the time. Simmer 2 minutes. Heat whisky until warm in small pan. Pour over venison and flame with a lighted match. Stir round and serve with boiled potatoes, extra redcurrant jelly and cooked sprouts or broccoli.

Venison or ostrich steaks in wine and breadcrumb sauce

SERVES 4

Club class. Eat with brown rice and any cooked vegetable you fancy.

1 tbsp sunflower oil
2 cloves of garlic, peeled
1 tbsp vegetable purée (paste)
1 tsp brown sugar
4 venison or ostrich steaks, washed and dried
150ml/^{1}/$_4$ pt/^{5}/$_8$ cup red wine
1 clementine, quartered
^{1}/$_2$ tsp salt or substitute
50g/2oz/1 cup soft white or brown breadcrumbs

1 Pour oil into a heavy-based frying pan and crush in garlic. Add vegetable purée (paste) with sugar then cook, stirring, over a medium heat for 2 to 3 minutes until hot.
2 Add steaks and fry 3 minutes per side. Pour in wine, bring to the boil then lower heat and cover.
3 Add clementine and salt. Re-cover and continue to simmer for 30 minutes.
4 Stir in crumbs and continue to cook, covered, for 2 minutes. Switch off heat and leave to stand a further 2 minutes before serving.

157

Quick step venison

SERVES 8

An incredibly fast way of cooking venison with only three main ingredients besides the meat. Eat with boiled potatoes tossed in chopped (minced) parsley and a dish of red cabbage which you can now buy canned in speciality food shops. Ostrich can be susbstituted for venison.

1 kg/2lb/32oz diced venison
$\frac{1}{2}$ packet (dry mix) French onion soup
$\frac{3}{4}$ litre/1 $\frac{1}{2}$ pt/3 $\frac{3}{4}$ cups water
Seasoning to taste

1 Wash venison and dry with paper towels. Dry-fry in a non-stick pan until each piece is well-sealed. The trick is to add meat gradually.
2 Mix in onion soup and water. Bring to the boil, stirring. Add seasoning to taste. Lower heat and cover.
3 Simmer over low heat for 1$\frac{1}{2}$ hours when meat should be soft, cooked through and moist.

PASTA, RICE AND GNOCCHI

Store cupboard vegetarian lasagne

SERVES 4 TO 6

With lasagne sheets you can use straight away without pre-cooking, plus tins and packets from the larder, you can put this together in about 10 minutes and come up with a true-to- life lasagne with an appetising golden brown crust.

1 can (about 400g/14oz/1$\frac{3}{4}$ cups) spinach purée
250g/9oz/1$\frac{1}{4}$ cups quark or fromage frais
$\frac{1}{4}$ tsp salt or substitute
2 large pinches grated nutmeg
10 lasagne sheets, each about 18 cm by 8 cm/7 inch by 3 inch
2 cans (EACH 375 to 400g/13oz to 14oz/about 2 cups) ratatouille
2 tbsp grated Parmesan cheese

1 Set oven to 180C/350F/Gas 4. Lightly oil a 23cm/9 inch square ovenproof dish or tin.
2 Drain spinach thoroughly through a fine mesh sieve, pressing it against sides with back of spoon to get rid of excess moisture. Tip into a bowl, combine with quark or fromage frais then season with salt and nutmeg.
3 Fill prepared dish alternately with layers of spinach mixture, lasagne sheets and the ratatouille.
4 Sprinkle with cheese and bake 50 minutes. Cut into portions, remove to warm plates and eat with salad.

Pappardelle pasta with mushrooms, tomato and apple

SERVES 4

A collector's piece for non-meat eaters in a hurry.

225g/8oz cup mushrooms
225g/8oz tomatoes, blanched
2 dessert apples
2 tsp sunflower oil
1 tsp garlic purée (paste)
1 tsp chopped (minced) basil
Salt or substitute
250g/9oz fresh pappardelle pasta flavoured with sun-dried tomatoes and
        herbs (or any other tomato pasta)
Boiling salted water

1 Trim mushrooms and wash. Wipe dry with paper towels. Roughly chop. Skin tomatoes. Peel, quarter and core apples then coarsely chop flesh.
2 Sizzle oil in a large frying pan. Add garlic purée (paste) and stir-fry over medium heat until golden.
3 Mix in mushrooms, tomatoes, apples, basil and salt to taste. Two-thirds cover pan and simmer 6 minutes.
4 Meanwhile cook pappardelle in boiling salted water as directed on the packet. Drain, return to pan and stand over low heat.
5 Add mushroom mixture and toss well with 2 spoons. Heat until bubbling, transfer to 4 warm plates and eat straight away.

Chinese spinach noodles with sprouting beans

SERVES 3 TO 4

It'll do your health good and goes with most other Chinese dishes.

250g/9oz Chinese noodles with spinach (pre-steamed, made by Blue
Dragon)
Boiling salted water
2 tsp sunflower oil
2 tsp garlic purée (paste)
150g/5oz sprouting beans
1 tsp medium Cantonese whole seed and curry spices (Schwartz)
¼ tsp salt or substitute

1 Cook noodles in boiling salted water as directed on the
  packet.
2 Meanwhile, sizzle oil in large frying pan. Add garlic purée
  (paste) and stir-fry over medium heat until golden.
3 Add sprouting beans, seed and spice blend and salt. Stir-fry 3
  minutes.
4 Drain noodles, return to saucepan and add bean sprout
  mixture. Toss with 2 spoons over a medium heat and serve
  very hot.

Extra red tomato pasta with roulé cheese sauce

Serves 4

A gourmet attraction with a light yet rich-tasting cream cheese and herb sauce.

3 medium tomatoes
2 medium red peppers (bell peppers)
Boiling water
8 spring onions (scallions)
2 tsp olive oil
100g/3 ½ oz Roulé light cream cheese with herbs
250g/9oz fresh tomato pasta
Boiling salted water
4 tsp grated Parmesan cheese

1 Put tomatoes into a fairly large bowl. Halve and de-seed peppers, put with tomatoes then add enough boiling water to cover both. Drain after 5 minutes.
2 Rinse under cold water. Skin tomatoes and chop. Roughly chop peppers. Trim onions (scallions) and also chop.
3 Heat oil in a fairly large and heavy-based frying pan until sizzling. Add onions and fry over medium heat $1\frac{1}{2}$ minutes. Add peppers, cover and continue to fry 5 minutes. Mix in tomatoes, cover again and simmer 3 minutes.
4 Cut Roulé cheese into small pieces and gradually work into vegetables, stirring all the time over low heat until melted. Cover and keep warm over low heat.
5 Cook pasta for about 5 minutes or according to pack directions. Drain and return to pan. Add the hot sauce and toss with 2 spoons until thoroughly mixed.
6 Serve on warm plates, sprinkling Parmesan lightly cheese over each portion.

Bucatini with mushroom and anchovy sauce

SERVES 3 TO 4

This pasta dish is characterised by a forthright sauce, distinctively Italian and near perfect with bucatini, a spaghetti look-alike but hollow in the middle - similar to drinking straws but thicker by a whisker. Preparation and cooking times are quite quick - no more than 15 to 20 minutes from start to finish.

200g/14oz bucatini (made by Barilla)
Boiling salted water
1 can (50g or just under 2oz) anchovy fillets in olive oil
2 to 3 cloves of garlic, peeeled
350g/12oz cup mushrooms
·3 tbsp chopped (minced) parsley, fresh or frozen
1 tbsp chopped (minced) basil, fresh or frozen

1 Cook bucatini in boiling salted water as directed on the packet
  – about 7 minutes.
2 Meanwhile tip anchovies with their oil into a small dish and
  finely mash. Crush in garlic then tip both into a fairly large
  frying pan,
3 Wash mushrooms, dry with paper towels then cut into
  medium-thick slices, stalks included if there are any.
4 Add to pan of anchovies and garlic, half cover with lid then
  simmer 5 minutes, stirring round twice with a spoon. Stir in
  parsley and basil.
5 Thoroughly drain bucatini and tip out on to warm plates. Top
  with mushroom sauce and serve very hot.

Genoese pasta with pesto and potatoes

An afterthought in a way and something I came across during a recent visit to the basil fields of Northern Italy and a tour of the Sacla factory to watch pesto being made by old and experienced hands who seemed to thrive on the heady scent of its distinctive quartet of ingredients- the basil itself, the Parmesan cheese, the pine nuts, the olive oil - in fact all the riches that go into this unique condiment. When we stopped for lunch en route near Genoa, we were given slender wiggly pasta tossed with pesto and small pieces of freshly cooked potatoes. It's a combination I'd never come across before until, about a month later, there it was again at London's famous Spaghetti House on the borders of Soho at a party to celebrate the restaurant's fortieth birthday. Called Pasta alla Genovese con Pesto e Patate in Italy, it's easy enough to make at home.

Cook enough pasta for 4 people and about 4 medium potatoes separately in salted water. It's a good idea to cut the potatoes into thickish pieces or slices first as they will cook more quickly. Drain both and add one to the other. Toss in just sufficient pesto to turn the pasta and potatoes pale green. Spoon out on to warm plates and dust each with about $1\frac{1}{2}$ teaspoons of Parmesan cheese. It makes a fulfilling meal without costing a fortune and is not too fat-laden.

Warm pizza-style macaroni

SERVES 4

A USA marathon with a hint of Italy, you can't go wrong with this store cupboard put-together, teamed with hot broccoli dusted with a scattering of grated Parmesan.

250g/8oz/2 cups macaroni
Boiling salted water
1 tsp olive oil
1 can (212g/7oz/1 cup) red salmon
1 can(285g/11oz/about 1 $\frac{1}{2}$ cups) mushrooms in brine
1 jar (200g/7oz/1 cup) sliced peppers in flavoured vinegar (called pizza
     garnish)
12 black olives without stones (pitted)
2 tbsp vegetable purée (paste)
1 clove of garlic, peeled and crushed
1 tbsp olive oil
3 heaped (heaping) tbsp chopped (minced) parsley

1 Cook macaroni in boiling salted water and oil as directed on the packet; about 8 to 9 minutes.
2 Meanwhile flake up salmon in its own liquor, removing black skin and bones. Drain mushrooms. Drain peppers, reserving vinegar. Halve olives lengthwise.
3 Strain macaroni and return to saucepan. Leave over minimal heat. Add mashed salmon, mushrooms, peppers and olives.
4 Beat together reserved pepper vinegar, vegetable purée (paste), garlic and oil. Pour on to macaroni, add parsley and toss all the ingredients gently together with 2 spoons.
5 Spoon out on to warm plates and serve straight away.

Rice stuffed aubergines (eggplant) with mixed vegetables

SERVES 4 AS A STARTER; 2 AS A MAIN COURSE

A hot climate specialty packed with nourishment, meaty-tasting yet totally vegetarian.

2 medium aubergines (eggplant)
A little sunflower oil
75g/3oz/$\frac{1}{2}$ cup brown rice
6 fluid oz/175ml/$\frac{3}{4}$ cup boiling salted water
2 medium onions
1 tbsp olive oil
1 medium red pepper (bell pepper)
2 cloves of garlic
1 medium celery stalk
2 medium tomatoes, blanched
3 tbsp chopped (minced) fresh or frozen parsley
Salt or substitute to taste
150ml/$\frac{1}{4}$ pt/$\frac{5}{8}$ cup boiling water

1 Set oven to 190C/375F/Gas 5. Wash and dry aubergines (eggplant) then score a line lengthwise along the centre of each (from pointed to rounded ends) with sharp knife. The slit will open up during baking and act as a cutting guide later on.
2 Put on to baking tray (cookie sheet) lined with lightly oiled foil. Brush aubergines (eggplant) thinly with more oil and bake for 45 minutes.
3 Meanwhile cook rice in boiling water as directed on page 175.
4 Peel onions and thinly slice. Separate slices into rings. Fry very slowly in saucepan with oil for about 15 minutes, keeping pan covered.
5 Halve pepper, removing inside fibres and seeds. Fairly finely chop flesh. Peel garlic and thinly slice. Well-wash celery, dry

with paper towels and cut into slender strips. Add all three to onions, mixing in well. Continue to fry,uncovered, for further 4 minutes.

6 Remove aubergines (eggplant) from oven, cool off slightly and halve along score lines. Scoop out flesh with spoon and coarsely chop on board. Add to vegetables in pan.

7 Skin tomatoes and chop. Drain rice. Add both to vegetable mixture with parsley and salt to taste. Stir in well.

8 Arrange aubergine (eggplant) shells in a baking dish. Fill with vegetable and rice mixture then pour in water. Bake 25 minutes and serve hot or cold.

Risotto with mushrooms

SERVES 4

Italy's answer to rice pudding, savoury instead of sweet, sometimes simmered with dried porcini mushrooms (known in France as cèpe) ,vegetable or meat stock, seasoning, wine and for our health-orientated purposes, only a prudent amount of Parmesan cheese. Older North Italians will tell you a proper Risotto, the genuine article, should be much richer than the one here, full of butter, bone marrow and impregnated with saffron and inordinate amounts of Parmesan cheese. That's how it used to be and they're right but youth in fashionable Italy is now remarkably health and weight conscious and my interpretation of the modern Risotto, even cooked in the microwave, is more in keeping with the ones we ate around the Italian Lakes two years' ago - much lighter in temperament than the vintage classics I remember from our travels in Tuscany during the seventies and eighties.

15g/$\frac{1}{2}$ oz dried porcini mushrooms (available from some supermarket
    chains)
3 tbsp dried onions
275ml/$\frac{1}{2}$ pt/1 $\frac{1}{4}$ cups boiling water
228g/8oz/1 cup Italian Arborio rice
450ml/16 fluid oz/2 cups warm vegetable stock
150ml/$\frac{1}{4}$ pt/$\frac{5}{8}$ cup dryish Italian white wine
$\frac{1}{2}$ to $\frac{3}{4}$ tsp salt or substitute
5 tbsp grated Parmesan cheese

1 Coarsely crumble mushrooms (which are fairly brittle) into a colander. Rinse under cold water then tip into a dish suitable for the microwave.
2 Mix in onions. Add boiling water, cover dish and leave to stand for 30 minutes. Add rice, stock, wine and salt. Stir round and cover with cling wrap. Slit twice to allow steam to escape and cook in a 650 watt microwave for 15 minutes at defrost setting.

3 Uncover and gently fork in 4 tablespoons cheese. Re-cover as before and cook at full power for 4$\frac{1}{2}$ to 5 minutes. When ready, the rice grains will be firm to the bite and the liquid thickish but not completely absorbed.
4 Spoon out on to 4 warm plates, sprinkle each lightly with remaining cheese and serve straight away, bearing in mind a freshly cooked risotto waits for no man; it congeals.

Potato gnocchi with mushrooms and mixed beans

SERVES 4 AS A STARTER

About 25 minutes is all it takes to put together an Italian creation with a myriad of flavours.

15g/$\frac{1}{2}$ oz dried porcini (cèpe) mushrooms
100ml/4 fluid oz/$\frac{1}{2}$ cup boiling water
1 jar (290g to 300g/12oz/1$\frac{1}{2}$ cups) mixed bean or artichoke antipasto
        in oil
$\frac{1}{2}$ tsp pesto
500g/1lb/16oz ready-prepared, shop-bought potato gnocchi
Boiling salted water

1 Wash dried mushrooms and soak in boiling water for 15 minutes. Drain.
2 Tip into saucepan with bean or artichoke antipasto. Bring slowly to boil and simmer gently, uncovered, 4 minutes. Stir in pesto.
3 Cook gnocchi in boiling salted water for 1 minute or as directed on the packet. Drain thoroughly.
4 Combine with the hot antipasto mixture, stirring gently until well combined. Serve straight away.

Leek and rice casserole

SERVES 4

A Balkan speciality with a hint of heat. It's designed for vegetarians or those inclined that way.

4 to 5 medium trimmed leeks, 8cm/3 inches green 'skirt' left on
Boiling salted water
4 tsp olive oil
75g/3oz/$^3/_8$ cup long grain rice
$^3/_4$ tsp salt or substitute
1 dried red chili
1 can (400g/14oz/1$^3/_4$ cups chopped tomatoes
125ml/$^1/_4$ pt/$^5/_8$ cup warm water
Juice of 1 large lemon

1 Lightly oil a fairly large ovenproof casserole. Trim and slit leeks then wash thoroughly between leaves to remove earth and grit. Cut into shortish chunks and cook in saucepan with boiling salted water for 6 minutes. Keep pan covered. Thoroughly drain. Rinse pan and wipe dry.
2 Heat oil in cleaned pan until sizzling. Add leeks and fry gently about 15 minutes until pale gold and beginning to tenderise.
3 Set oven to 190C/375F/Gas 5. Spoon leeks into prepared casserole then sprinkle with rice and salt. Add chilli.
4 Spoon tomatoes and liquid from can evenly over the top then gently pour water down side of dish.
5 Cover securely and bake 30 to 40 minutes until rice is cooked. Uncover, sprinkle with lemon juice and serve while still piping hot.

♥

Gnocchi with leek sauce

SERVES 4 AS A STARTER

An outstanding meal starter whether you use potato gnocchi or pasta like penne or macaroni.

2 medium leeks
2 tbsp olive oil
6 tsp black olive paté (paste), shop-bought
4 tbsp dry Italian white wine
1 tbsp vegetable purée (paste)
500g/1lb/16oz potato gnocchi
Boiling salted water

1 Trim leeks, leaving on about 8cm/3-inches green 'skirt'. Slit lengthwise then wash thoroughly between leaves to remove earth and grit. Shake dry and cut into narrow rings.
2 Heat oil in saucepan until it just begins to sizzle. Add leeks, mix in well then cover pan. Fry gently for 10 minutes, stirring 3 times.
3 Uncover and stir in olive paté (paste), wine and vegetable purée (paste). Bring just up to the boil, reduce heat to minimum and cover.
4 Cook gnocchi in the boiling salted water for 1 minute or as directed on the packet. Drain thoroughly, add to leek mixture and toss gently to mix. Spoon on to warm plates and serve straight away.

Tip:
If substituting pasta for gnocchi, use 225g/8oz.

GRAINS

Basmati rice

Always used by Indian cooks, Basmati is a long-grained, slender rice which cooks to perfection if you follow the technique given to me by Terry Butcher of Tolly Boy rice. The company's Basmati is sold under the brand name of Guru which cooks up to a dream-like splendour of whitness, every grain separate, every grain dry. Better still, his cooking method works with most other kinds of rice as well.

Basic rice

SERVES 4

Tip 1 large cup or mug of Basmati rice into saucepan. Add $\frac{1}{2}$ to 1 tsp salt or substitute and 1 $\frac{1}{2}$ cups or mugs of COLD water: alternatively, and if you prefer specific measures, tip 225g/8oz/1 cup rice into saucepan. Add 450ml/16 fluid oz or 2 cups COLD water. Bring to boil, at once lower heat to minimum and tightly cover. Simmer for EXACTLY 15 minutes without lifting lid. Switch off heat, stand for 2 minutes then uncover, fork round and serve.

Microwaving (650 watt)
The same ratio as above. Cook in covered dish for 12 minutes at full power. Stand 5 minutes, fork round and serve.

American long grain

Prepare and cook as above.

Brown

Prepare and cook as Basmati rice but allow 20 minutes and not 15.

Brown and wild rice

SERVES 4

Brown rice is unprocessed with only the husk removed, leaving the healthy bran intact. Wild rice is not a rice at all but the dark brown, elongated and slim seed of a special cultivated grass growing in parts of North America and China. Put the two together and the combination is dramatic.

50g/2oz/about $^3/_8$ cup wild rice
175g/6oz/about $^7/_8$ cup brown rice
450ml/16 fluid oz/2 cups cold vegetable stock or water
$^1/_2$ to 1 tsp salt or substitute

1 Put all ingredients into saucepan. Bring to the boil, stirring once or twice with fork.
2 Lower heat to minimum and cover tightly.
3 Cook 25 minutes without lifting lid. Switch off heat and leave to stand 4 minutes before forking round and serving.

Polenta (cornmeal)

SERVES 4

The 'in' thing in trendy Italian restaurants and Romania's national side dish (called Mamaliga), polenta is a deeply yellow, almost honey-flavoured grain which cooks up into a smooth and thick savoury 'pudding', a star attraction moulded and sliced cold then grilled or fried or, for simpler souls, spooned out on to plates and served steaming hot with egg, poultry and some vegetarian dishes. The way I cook mine, starting with cold water, seems to prevent lumps though packet directions suggest you use hot. It's up to you.

<u>Basic Polenta:</u>
575ml/1 $\frac{1}{4}$ pt/2 $\frac{1}{2}$ cups cold water
1 tsp salt or substitute
125g/4oz/$\frac{5}{8}$ cup polenta

1 Put all ingredients into a heavy-based pan, non-sick for preference.
2 Slowly bring to boil, stirring continuously, until mixture just begins to boil.
3 Two-thirds cover pan with lid to prevent spluttering and simmer about 6 minutes, stirring twice.
4 Spoon out on to warm plates and eat with the meal.

Polenta with sun-dried tomato paste

Ripple 1 to 2 teaspoons of the paste into each portion. For an all-over orange colour, stir 2 to 3 tablespoons of the paste into the polenta while it's still in the pan.

Polenta with pesto

Stir $\frac{1}{2}$ tsp into each portion.

Cous-cous

This is basically durum wheat semolina, expertly converted into tiny and perfectly rounded balls which resemble millet or tapioca in appearance although are smaller - almost like seed pearls. Traditionally steamed over the simmering pot of stew in a muslin-lined colander or in the top of a couscousière (a double pan with a steamer on top), the French have come up with an altogether easier and more practical method of cooking the grains. It does away with steaming completely and takes about 5 minutes to do in a conventional saucepan.

650ml/1pt/20 fluid oz/2$^3/_4$ cup boiling water
50g/2oz/$^3/_8$ cup raisins
$^1/_2$ tsp saffron strands
500g/18oz/just over 2 cups packeted Cous-Cous
25g/1oz/about $^1/_4$ cup flaked and toasted almonds

1 Pour water into large pan with raisins. Bring back to boil and simmer, uncovered, for 2 minutes. Add saffron. Cover and leave to stand, off heat, for 5 minutes.
2 Bring up to the boil again and remove from heat. Tip in the Cous-Cous and fork round as lightly as you can. Cover and stand 3 minutes.
3 Fork round lightly again, this time with almonds. Serve straight away.

Tip:
Leftovers can be frozen then de-frosted, reheated and served hot with any other kind of stew.

♥

Barley

SERVES 4

An old-fashioned grain used in soups, broths and stews and underrated for its value in the diet, research in the USA some six or seven years' ago claimed it inhibited the liver's production of bad cholesterol or LDL (see page 13) and helped to prevent veins and arteries from becoming clogged and furred up. We should obviously eat it more. If you are looking for something with a difference, have a go with my Barley Bread on page 210, or for a side dish to support main courses instead of the more usual potatoes, rice or pasta, cooked barley flakes offer a Middle European alternative. It's a slightly chewy cereal with an 'al dente' feel to it and has a snug, nutty taste.

Basic barley flakes

125g/4oz/about 2 cups barley flakes (from health food shops)
575ml/1pt/2 $\frac{1}{2}$ cups cold water
1 vegetable stock cube

1 Tip barley flakes into saucepan and pour in water. Crumble in stock cube.
2 Bring to the boil, stirring. Lower heat and cover. simmer slowly 15 minutes, stirring twice.

Quinoa

Pronounced keenowa, this is a fascinating grain from Peru with a bitey texture and somewhat curious flavour - almost smokey like China tea. Highly-prized by the early Incas, quinoa is a healthy and nutritious food containing 14.9g of protein per 100g and 8.0g of fibre and is a comparatively new-on-the-scene cereal, appropriate for serving as a side dish with almost any savoury dish except curry. As it is bland, you can use vegetable stock for cooking instead of water. Quinoa is available from most health food shop chains.

Basic quinoa

SERVES 4

125g/4oz/about $^5/_8$ cup quinoa
350ml/14 fluid oz/1 $^3/_4$ cups cold water or vegetable stock
$^1/_4$ tsp salt or substitute

1 Put all ingredients into saucepan and bring to the boil, stirring.
2 Lower heat and cover securely. Simmer about 12 to 15 minutes until all or most of the liquid is absorbed. Drain if necessary and eat straight away.

Quinoa with pine nuts

Stir 4 tablespoons lightly toasted pinenuts (kernels) after cooking. The grain and nuts complement each other brilliantly.

Buckwheat

Essentially Middle European, Jewish and Japanese , cooked buckwheat stays firm to the bite at all times, tastes of roasted hazelnuts and goes with bold and gutsy stews of venison, turkey, rabbit, hare and pheasant, anything edible containing beetroot (beets), mushrooms and aubergines (eggplant) in any shape or form. Unrelated to any other grain, buckwheat (also known as beechwheat or Saracen corn) is native to Russia and is the small fruit of a pink-flowering and sweet-scented plant (Latin, Fagopyrum esculentum) which is a member of the dock family. The grains, typically three-cornered and on a par in size to pearl barley, are sold in health food shops already husked and sometimes toasted. Brought to Europe by the Crusaders, buckwheat is a Russian and Polish staple (where it is known as kasha) and eaten as a breakfast cereal with milk and sugar and also added to soups, stews and stuffings. Russia apart, buckwheat is grown in parts of North America (and known as buckwheat groats), France, Germany, Eastern Europe, China and Japan. When converted into flour, the Japanese use it to make buff-coloured noodles and the Russians their famous blinis or pancakes. Buckwheat is an excellent source of vitamin B and valuable protein and its rutic acid content is believed to be beneficial to those with coronary heart disease. It is both wheat and gluten-free.

Basic buckwheat

SERVES 4

175g/6oz/about 1 cup buckwheat
675ml/1 ¼ pt/3 cups boiling water
1 tsp salt or substitute

1 Put buckwheat into a sturdy frying pan or saucepan and toast by dry-frying for about 4 minutes until grains are brown. Stir frequently.
2 Gradually pour in water. Add salt. Cover closely and cook over medium heat for 20 minutes, stirring twice.

Flavoured buckwheat

SERVES 4

Make as above, adding 3 tablespoons dried onion flakes with water. After 10 minutes, add 125g/4oz cleaned and sliced wild or ordinary mushrooms, stir-fried for 6 minutes in 2 teaspoons sunflower oil.

Millet

Often regarded as bird seed in the West, millet is an important cereal in parts of Asia and Africa and a grain which pre-dates rice as a staple food in China. Related to sorghum, it is yellow in colour, seed-like to look at and absorbs four times its own weight of water. The taste of millet is mild and delicate, reminiscent of cracked wheat and cornmeal combined, and can be used as a substitute for rice and sometimes small pasta (pastini). When eaten with pulses (peas, beans or lentils), it makes a nutritionally sound and well-balanced protein meal. Millet is an annual crop, Latin name Panicum milliaceum.

Basic millet

SERVES 4 TO 6

175g/6oz/about $^3/_4$ cup millet
$^3/_4$ litre/1 $^1/_4$ pt/3 cups boiling water
1 vegetable stock cube (optional)
$^1/_2$ tsp salt or substitute

1 Put millet into a heavy-based, non-stick pan and dry-fry until toasted and popping noises emerge. This can take anything from 5 to 10 minutes depending on thickness of pan and type of heat. Stir frequently so that millet browns evenly.
2 Add water then crumble in stock cube if used. Fork in salt, bring to the boil, lower heat and cover tightly with well-fitting lid.
3 Cook 20 to 25 minutes until millet has absorbed all the water and looks puffed-up and fluffy.
4 Fork round and serve piping hot.

PUDDINGS

Bramley bumbles with redcurrant meringue

SERVES 4

Nursery food for grown-ups!

575g/1 $\frac{1}{4}$ lb Bramley or other sour cooking apples
3 tbsp water
1 tbsp thick honey
1 can (425g/15oz/about 2 cups) low fat Devon custard
125g/4oz/about $\frac{3}{4}$ cup redcurrants, removed from stalks

Topping
3 size 3 egg whites
Squeeze of lemon
75g/3oz/ $\frac{3}{8}$ cup caster (superfine) sugar

1 Peel, core and slice apples. Put into saucepan with water. Bring to boil, lower heat and cover. Cook over a medium heat until apples puff up in the pan like a souffle and are very soft.
2 Beat until smooth, add honey then blend in custard. Set oven to 180C/350F/Gas 4. Divide between 4 lightly oiled ovenproof dishes. Wash redcurrants, pat dry with paper towels and leave on one side for time being.
3 Beat egg whites and lemon juice to a stiff and snowy foam. Gradually add sugar and continue beating until meringue is thick, heavy and stands in firm peaks when beaters are lifted out of bowl.
4 Fold in redcurrants then pile equal amounts of meringue over apple puddings. Bake about 15 minutes until lightly golden brown. Eat hot.

Malt loaf and marmalade pudding

SERVES 8

*Man's best friend. A splodgy, spicy, sticky, wicked-tasting pudding
reminiscent of all the riches of Christmas. Only this one's harmless provided
you bypass cream or ice cream and eat with lightly warmed apple sauce,
skimmed condensed milk (Fussell's) or just-beginning-to-melt fruit sorbet.*

675g to 700g/1 $\frac{1}{2}$ lb/ 24oz malt loaf (fatless)
275ml/$\frac{1}{2}$ pt/1 $\frac{1}{4}$ cups very hot tea, strained
1 $\frac{1}{2}$ tsp mixed spice (allspice)
1 $\frac{1}{2}$ tsp cinnamon
2 tbsp sunflower oil
6 generous tbsp coarse cut orange marmalade
2 tbsp light brown soft sugar

1 Lightly oil an oblong heatproof dish (pan) measuring about
   25cm by 15 cm by 4 cm/10-inch by 6-inch by 1$\frac{1}{2}$ inches. Set
   oven to 160C/325F/Gas 3.
2 Break up loaf, put into mixing bowl and add all remaining
   ingredients. Stand 5 minutes then beat until smooth.
3 Spread smoothly into dish (pan) and bake, uncovered, for 1
   hour. Spoon out on plates and eat warm or cold but not
   chilled.

Ice blush sorbet

SERVES 8 TO 10

With a hint of pink and a smooth, soft and scoopable texture, this is a debonair sorbet for special times. Leftovers freeze perfectly.

175g/6oz/^{3}/$_4$ cup caster (superfine) sugar
150ml/^{1}/$_4$ pt/^{5}/$_8$ cup cold water
1 standard size bottle of rosé wine (Portuguese Mateus works well)
1 envelope/3 tsp powdered gelatine
75ml/3 fluid oz/^{3}/$_8$ cup cold water
1 tsp vanilla essence (extract)
3 whites from large eggs
^{1}/$_4$ tsp lemon juice
50g/2oz/^{1}/$_4$ cup caster (superfine) sugar

1 Put sugar and water into heavy-based saucepan. Stand over low heat and leave until sugar has completely dissolved and liquid is clear. Stir 2 or 3 times.
2 Continue to bubble gently, uncovered, until mixture thickens slightly and becomes syrupy. On NO account allow to turn golden.
3 Draw pan away from heat, cool for 5 minutes then gradually pour in wine.
4 Transfer to large bowl, cover securely and chill in the freezer until sorbet has frozen 5 cm/2 inches round sides of bowl.
5 Meanwhile, tip gelatine into small pan, add second amount of cold water, stand for 3 minutes then melt over low heat. Stir in vanilla.
6 Whisk egg whites and lemon juice until stiff and snow-like then gradually whisk in sugar to make a thick and shiny meringue.
7 Whisk sorbet until light and all the ice crystals broken down. Gradually beat in one third of the meringue and liquid gelatine.
8 Smoothly fold in rest of meringue with large metal spoon then cover and freeze 2 hours. Re-whisk, cover and freeze about 8 hours until firm. Scoop into dishes to serve.

Sorbet sundaes

EACH SERVES 4

All the sundaes are fresh and fruity, glorious in the summer, cheerfully decorative. Unlike ice cream, sorbet is fatless and one of the safe luxuries of life. All sorbets for these recipies have been shop bought.

Iced Pink Grapefruit
Fill 4 deepish wine glasses with scoops of pink grapefruit sorbet, trickling in green creme de menthe at the same time. Decorate with fresh mint leaves.

Palm Beach
Fill 4 medium tall sundae glasses with alternate scoops of mango and peach sorbets, adding spoons of coulis (page 93) at the same time. Decorate with orange slices.

Cold Snap
Fill 4 deepish wine glasses with scoops of lemon sorbet, pouring in a thin stream of ruby port at the same time. Decorate with deep red cherries, left on their stalks.

Bohemia
Fill 4 medium tall sundae glasses with scoops of blackcurrant sorbet, adding crushed and sweetened fresh strawberries at the same time. You'll need about 225g/8oz/2 cups. Decorate with whole raspberries.

Golden Desert
Fill 4 medium tall sundae glasses with scoops of pineapple sorbet, adding random slices of peeled kiwi fruit and drizzle of orange liqueur. Decorate with fresh peach slices brushed with lemon juice.

Forest Flowers
Fill 4 medium tall sundae glasses with scoops of peach sorbet, adding a little elderflower cordial at the same time.

Scented fruits

SERVES 6 TO 8

There is something unique about this haunting and unorthodox fruit salad, the ultimate surprise.

225g/8oz/1 $\frac{1}{2}$ cups dried apricot halves
275ml/ $\frac{1}{2}$ pt/1 $\frac{1}{4}$ cups strong tea, freshly brewed
6 tbsp dark clear honey
225g/8oz/about 2 cups fresh dates (like Israeli Carmel)
1 medium fresh pineapple
2 tbsp orange flower water (order from your local pharmacy)
3 tbsp cointreau

1 Rinse apricots under cold running water then scissor-snip each into 4 pieces.
2 Put into saucepan with tea and honey. Simmer, uncovered, 10 minutes but do not allow to boil rapidly.
3 Meanwhile, skin dates and cut in half, removing stones. Peel pineapple, lifting out eyes with tip of potato peeler. Cut into slices then cut each slice into small triangles without removing core.
4 Add both to pan of apricots with last two ingredients. Cover and cool. Refrigerate about 1 hour before serving.

Sorbet sauce fruit compote

Serves 4 to 6

Cool right through.

2 nectarines
2 peaches
225g to 250g/8oz/2 cups fresh strawberries, rinsed and drained
175g/6oz/about 1 $\frac{1}{4}$ cups fresh blackberries or black seedless grapes, rinsed
    and drained
$\frac{1}{4}$ litre (about 9oz or $\frac{1}{4}$ tub) shop-bought blueberry or other berry sorbet
3 tbsp fruit flavoured liqueur

To serve
Low fat fromage frais

1 Put nectarines and peaches into bowl and cover with boiling
   water. Leave 2 minutes then drain. Cover with cold water.
2 When lukewarm, drain again and peel each piece of fruit.
   Halve, remove stones and dice flesh with a stainless knife. Put
   into a crystal or plain glass serving bowl.
3 Slice strawberries and add to bowl with blackberries or grapes.
   Add sorbet and stir gently until it melts completely and forms
   a sauce.
4 Stir in liqueur and serve while still very cold with the fromage
   frais.

Summer custard fruit and bun pudding

SERVES 4

Twixt and between a trifle and summer pudding.

225g/8oz/about 2 cups EACH strawberries and raspberries
3 fruit buns
8 tbsp sweet sherry or grape juice
575ml/1pt/2½ cups freshly-prepared custard (vanilla sauce) made with
    skimmed milk
Sugar or powdered substitute to taste

1 Wash both fruits and gently pat dry with paper towels. Keep aside 4 of the best strawberries and 8 raspberries for decoration.
2 Halve buns and arrange all the bases, cut sides up, in a fairly shallow oblong dish of 1½ litre/2½ pint capacity. Moisten with half the sherry or grape juice.
3 Sweeten custard (vanilla sauce) to taste then spoon half the amount over buns. Spread with half the fruit and sprinkle with sugar or substitute.
4 Top with rest of buns, again cut sides facing, and sprinkle with remaining sherry or grape juice. Add a final layer of fruit and coat with balance of custard. Cool and chill at least 2 hours. Decorate with reserved fruit before serving.

Tip
Make custard (vanilla sauce) following directions on packet. If more convenient, buy ready-made in cans or tetrapaks.

Deepest red fruit salad

SERVES 4 TO 6

Lucious and a dark rich red, the addition of elderflower cordial makes a subtle difference to the fruit, adding a new dimension to the already exquisite taste. Serve solo or with any of the low fat dairy products - yogurt, fromage frais, skimmed condensed milk (Fussel's), quark or custard (vanilla sauce).

150g to 175g/6 to 7oz/about 1 ¹/₂ cups fresh blueberries
150ml/¹/₄ pt/⁵/₈ cup cold water
2 tbsp granulated sugar
450g to 500g/1lb/4 cups ripe strawberries
3 tbsp elderflower cordial

1 Wash blueberries and put into pan with water. Bring to boil, lower heat and cover. Simmer gently for 5 to 7 minutes until soft.
2 Add sugar and stir lightly until melted. Leave to cool. Wash strawberries and carefully pat dry. Halve lengthwise and add to the cold blueberry mixture with cordial.
3 Mix well with a spoon. Transfer to a fancy glass bowl and cover. Refrigerate about 2 hours before serving.

Espresso chestnut paté

SERVES 6

A silken, high flying contribution for pudding addicts.

1 can (439g/15$\frac{1}{2}$ oz/2 cups) unsweetened chestnut purée (Clement
    Faugier)
5 tbsp icing (confectioner's) sugar
1 individual sachet of instant espresso coffee powder
2 tbsp hot water
2 tbsp coffee liqueur (such as Kahlua or Tia Maria)
2 whites from large eggs
Pinch of salt
About 1 tsp cocoa powder

1 Put chestnut purée into a bowl and break down with fork. Beat
    in icing sugar followed by coffee dissolved in hot water. Stir in
    coffee liqueur.
2 Whip egg whites to stiff snow with salt then fold into chestnut
    mixture with large metal spoon or spatula. When smoothly
    combined, spread evenly into 6 ramekin dishes and chill for
    about 2 hours.
3 Before serving, sift cocoa over top of each. Eat with a spoon.

Pomegranates with flowers

SERVES 6

Glistening beads of pomegranate, macerated in orange flower water and citrus cordial, is a variation on a Middle Eastern theme, sensual, a visual feast, exquisitely light and refreshing. Serve in glass bowls to do full justice to the jewelled colour effect and add a shot of cassis or blackcurrant syrup to each to deepen the flavour.

5 or 6 pomegranates, washed and dried
3 tbsp citrus cordial (made by Bottle Green)
2 tbsp orange flower water (from pharmacies)

1 Cut pomegranates into quarters. Holding each quarter over a bowl, bend the skin back on itself and ease out the seeds with fingers or a teaspoon. Avoid dropping in pieces of coarse yellow pith which are bitter.
2 Stir in remaining ingredients. Cover and refrigerate 2 to 3 hours before serving.

Marsala mulled peaches

SERVES 4

Quite beautiful.

4 large peaches
150ml/$\frac{1}{4}$ pt/$\frac{5}{8}$ cup marsala
150ml/$\frac{1}{4}$ pt/$\frac{5}{8}$ cup water
4 tbsp brown sugar
2 cloves
5 cm/2 inch piece of cinnamon stick
Juice of $\frac{1}{2}$ lemon
1 tsp vanilla essence (extract)

1 Put peaches into a dish or bowl in a single layer. Prick skin of each once with tip of knife then blanch by covering with boiling water.
2 Leave for 3 minutes and drain. Cover with cold water and strain when peaches are cool enough to handle. Slide off skins.
3 Pour marsala and water into saucepan. Add sugar and stir over medium heat until dissolved. Mix in all remaining ingredients, including peaches.
4 Cover and simmer peaches 10 minutes, turning over once with large spoon. Transfer peaches to 4 fancy dessert dishes and coat each with the marsala sauce.

Strawberry and orange will-o-the wisp

SERVES 4

A feather-light sweet for midsummer when strawberries are in full swing.

1 packet orange flavour jelly
4 tbsp boiling water
275g/10oz/about 1 $\frac{1}{2}$ cups ripe strawberries
Ice cubes
Whites from 2 large eggs
Squeeze of lemon juice

1　Divide jelly into cubes and put into a small saucepan with water. Leave over low heat until melted but don't allow to boil. Take off heat.
2　Wash and drain strawberries and gently pat dry with paper towels. Reserve 4 of the best looking berries for decoration. Crush remainder in measuring cup.
3　Gradually whisk in melted jelly then make up to 575ml/1 pint/2 $\frac{1}{2}$ cups with ice cubes. Stir without stopping until the cubes have melted and jelly begins to thicken. Transfer to the fridge.
4　In a clean, dry and fairly large bowl, beat egg whites and lemon juice together until they form a firm and fluffy snow.
5　Gradually whisk still semi-liquid jelly mixture into whites. When smoothly-combined, spoon into 4 dessert dishes and chill until firm.
6　Decorate each with a strawberry before serving.

Coconut and lemon bubble

SERVES 4

An easy option for a light-hearted, fluffy sweet made from a handful of ingredients. With a tinge of the tropics, this is heaven-sent for summer, totally original and stylish when decorated with seasonal soft fruits or a spoon or two of coulis (page 93).

1 packet lemon flavour jelly
1 can (400ml/14 fluid oz/1 $^{3}/_{4}$ cups coconut milk
2 whites from large eggs
Squeeze of lemon juice
50g/2oz/$^{1}/_{4}$ cup Greek style thick yogurt

1 Divide jelly into cubes and put into saucepan with coconut milk. Stir over minimal heat until jelly melts but DO NOT ALLOW TO BOIL. Remove from heat and cool.
2 Pour into a dish, cover with plate and refrigerate until just beginning to thicken and set round the edges.
3 Whip egg whites stiffly with lemon juice. Whip one-third into jelly mixture.
4 Using a large metal spoon or plastic spatula, fold rest of beaten whites into jelly alternately with yogurt. Transfer to 4 dessert dishes and refrigerate until softly set before serving.

Date and apricot pots

SERVES 6

A typically English pudding made with dried fruits instead of fresh, cheered on its way with cider and 'creamed' with yogurt. A hint. You'll need a sturdy food processor for mixing.

225g/8oz/1 $\frac{1}{3}$ cups dried apricots
175g/6oz/1 cup chopped dried dates
275ml/$\frac{1}{2}$ pt/1 $\frac{1}{4}$ cups medium sweet cider
300g/11oz/1 $\frac{3}{8}$ cup Greek yogurt (light)
2 tbsp chopped (minced) pistachio nuts for decoration

1 Well-wash apricots then scissor-snip into small pieces. Put into fairly large bowl and add dates.
2 Bring cider just up to the boil. Pour over fruit, cover and leave to stand for 4 hours.
3 To complete, work apricots, dates and cider to a thickish purée in a food processor.
4 With machine still running, add yogurt gradually then pulse until ingredients form a thickish and slightly coarse purée.
5 Spoon into 6 ramekin dishes or small pottery or glass pots and chill for several hours in the refrigerator. Before serving, sprinkle tops with nuts.

Apple pie pudding

SERVES 4

A pudding in the fast lane, made with only three ingredients.

1 can (397g/about 14oz/1$^{3}/_{4}$ cups) spiced apple and raisin fruit filling
225g/about 8oz/1 cup sheeps' milk yogurt
4 tsp demerara sugar (coarse brown sugar)
4 sponge finger biscuits for serving

1 Tip fruit filling into bowl and gradually stir in yogurt.
2 Spoon into 4 dessert dishes and refrigerate until well-chilled.
3 Sprinkle each with sugar before serving and accompany with biscuits.

Black cherry and ginger jelly

SERVES 4

Garnet-coloured adult jellies fired with ginger wine and flavoured with lemon - fabulous and made in under 10 minutes.

1 pkt of black cherry jelly
Water
Juice of 1 medium lemon
Ginger wine

<u>To serve</u>
4 tsp crème fraîche
Cinnamon

1 Divide jelly into cubes (cutting with scissors is practical) and put into glass or plastic measuring cup. Make up to 425ml/$\frac{3}{4}$ pt/2 cups with water.
2 Melt for a few minutes at defrost setting in the microwave (or in saucepan over low heat). Stir in lemon juice then make up to 575ml/1pint/2$\frac{1}{2}$ cups with ginger wine.
3 Pour into 4 glass dessert dishes and refrigerate until set.
4 Top each with teaspoon of crème fraîche before serving and dust with cinnamon.

Poached pears in grape juice with amaretto

SERVES 4

Another one from Swan's Slow Cooker, cleverly flavoured with almondy amaretto liqueur from Italy. You can serve the pears plain as they are or with yogurt or light crème fraîche.

40g/1 $\frac{1}{2}$ oz/just over $\frac{1}{8}$ cup caster (superfine) sugar
575ml/1 pt/2 $\frac{1}{2}$ cups sparkling red grape juice
2 cinnamon sticks
4 large firm pears
2 to 3 tbsp amaretto

1　Preheat the slow cooker then add sugar, grape juice and cinnamon sticks. Stir well to mix.
2　Peel and quarter the pears. Remove cores, leaving stalks in place where possible. Halve each quarter of pear lengthwise and add to the cooker.
3　Mix round, gently pushing pears under the surface of the liquid. Cover and cook on high for 4 to 6 hours or on automatic for 5 to 7 hours.
4　Stir once or twice during cooking. Mix in amaretto and chill before serving.

Tip
The main advantage of a slow cooker is its low running costs.

Carrot curd

MAKES ABOUT 1KG (2$\frac{1}{4}$ LB/4$\frac{1}{2}$ CUPS)

As fragrant as an armful of country flowers, blessed with an abundance of Vitamin A and coloured deep amber, this incredible and eggless carrot curd makes a stunning substitute for butter-laden lemon or orange curd. Besides being used as a spread on all things toasted, it is absolutely delicious with roast poultry and game and goes perfectly with grilled venison and turkey breast steaks. Take heed though. It's on the sweet side and a little goes a long way.

1kg/2.2lb/34oz carrots
275ml/$\frac{1}{2}$ pt/1$\frac{1}{4}$ cups water
2 cloves
450g/1lb/2 cups light brown soft sugar
Finely grated peel and juice of 2 medium lemons

1 Peel carrots and coarsely grate, either by hand or in a food processor.
2 Transfer to fairly large saucepan. Stir in water and cloves. Bring to boil, stirring. Lower heat, cover tightly then simmer over low heat for 50 minutes. Take out cloves.
3 Add sugar, lemon peel with juice and stir until melted. Bring just up to the boil (careful - the mixture splutters), two-thirds cover with lid and simmer slowly for 1$\frac{1}{4}$ hours until curd is thick and dark orange in colour.
4 Cool to lukewarm, spoon into warm jars and leave until cold. Cover as you would jam and store in the refrigerator.

Lemon mousse

SERVES 4 TO 6

Short of time, economising, entertaining? Here's a brilliant solution for hot days, a one-in-a-million pudding with a smooth and flawless texture, blissfully soft, light on riches, intensely lemon.

1 can (450 g) Fussell's skimmed sweetened condensed milk
Finely grated peel and juice of 2 large lemons
2 egg whites from size 2 eggs
Pinch of salt
Mint for decoration

1 Tip milk into a mixing bowl and add lemon peel and juice. Stir briefly, without beating, until thickened.
2 Separately whisk egg and salt into a stiff snow. Beat one-third into the lemon mixture then gently fold in remainder with a large metal spoon.
3 Divide between individual glass dishes and chilli before serving. Decorate with sprigs of mint.

BREADS

Sun-dried tomato and olive bread

MAKES 2 LOAVES

At first glance, and if you didn't know, you'd think you were looking at a fruit cake rather than an Italian style loaf but one bite and you realize straight away from the flavours of the sun-dried tomatoes, black olives and basil that you're into the Med scene in a big way. I've adapted it from a recipe given to me by a brainy lady called Topsi Ventner who runs the Roggeland Country House hotel in Northern Paarl, part of the Cape Province of South Africa. We wined and dined magnificently during our stay at this superb specimen of an old Cape Dutch tavern set against a backdrop of multi-coloured mountains and semi-tropical flora and fauna, and on those rare occasions when we weren't eating and when Topsi had a few moments to spare in between flower arranging, pandering to her assortment of cats and dogs and cooking for guests, we'd sit down in her vast kitchen, drink endless cups of coffee, exchange recipes and gossip about mutual contacts from both our countries. It was time well spent. Now the recipe.

750g/1 ½ lb/6 cups strong plain (all-purpose) flour, white or brown
1 tsp salt or substitute
1 sachet easy blend dried yeast
50g/2oz sundried tomatoes in olive oil (largish pieces)
20 black olives without stones (pitted)
2 tsp dried basil
425ml/15 fluid oz/ about 2 cups lukewarm (tepid) water which equates to
    blood heat

1 Sift flour and salt into large mixing bowl. Toss in yeast.
2 Take tomatoes out of oil and roughly chop. Slice olives into
   rings. Add both to flour with basil and gently toss again.
3 Add water in one go, stir into dry ingredients with fork and
   keep stirring until mixture sticks together into a clumpy
   dough. Take out of bowl, put on to floured work surface and

knead about 10 to 15 minutes until it is smooth, elastic and no longer sticky. If dough stays tacky, work in a little extra flour.

4 Shape dough into a ball and put into a clean and lightly oiled bowl, fairly large in size. Cover with a piece of oiled plastic wrap and leave dough to rise in the kitchen for 2 to 3 hours (maybe longer in the depths of winter) until it doubles in size.

5 Return to floured work surface and quickly knead flat (known as punching down). Cut in half, shape into two 15cm/6 inch rounds and transfer to large baking tray (cookie sheet), first oiled and floured. If preferred, shape into oblongs and put into 2 by 1kg (2lb or 32oz) oiled and floured loaf tins (pans) .

6 Cover loosely with oiled foil and leave to rise until dough doubles in size in the case of the round loaves, or reaches tops of tins (pans). Uncover. Bake 20 minutes in oven preheated to 230C/450F/Gas 8.

7 Turn round loaves over on their own baking tray (cookie sheet) and crispen in the oven for 10 minutes when bases should be dry and golden. For loaves in tins, turn out on to baking tray (cookie sheet) and also bake upside down a further 10 minutes. Cool on wire rack and store in a bread bin for 2-3 days when cold.

Pesto bread

MAKES 2 LOAVES.

Bread with soul.

Follow above recipe, substituting 3 tablespoons red or green pesto for sundried tomatoes and olives. Dough may need an extra tablespoon or so of flour to make it firm.

Onion bread with cummin

Makes 1 loaf

A tasty contribution and a bread that does wonders to cheer up bland foods like cottage cheese and fromage frais. It's also superb sliced and toasted then topped with baked beans, canned spaghetti in tomato sauce or grilled mushrooms - even a couple of rashers (strips) of the leanest grilled bacon you can find.

25g/1oz/$\frac{1}{4}$ cup dried onions
2 tbsp sunflower oil
225g/8oz/1$\frac{3}{4}$ to 2 cups strong white plain flour (all-purpose)
1 tsp salt or substitute
2 tsp ground cummin
225g/8oz/1$\frac{3}{4}$ to 2 cups strong wholemeal plain flour (graham flour)
1 sachet easy blend dried yeast
350ml/12oz 1$\frac{1}{2}$ cups lukewarm (tepid) water
1 extra tblsp sunflower oil

1 Put onions and first amount of oil into pan and fry gently until onions turn pale golden brown. Watch carefully as they easily burn. Take pan off heat.
2 Sift white flour into bowl with salt and cummin then toss in wholemeal flour, yeast and fried onions with oil.
3 Mix to dough with water and remaining oil then turn out on to floured surface and knead 10 to 12 minutes. By this time, dough should be smooth and stretchy but if it remains on the sticky side, work in a little extra white flour.
4 Shape into a ball and put into a fairly large mixing bowl, first lightly oiled. Cover with oiled plastic wrap and leave in a warm area - airing cupboard, above an Aga type cooker etc - until dough doubles in size.
5 Return to floured work surface and quickly knead flat (known

as punching down). Shape into an oblong and drop into 1kg/ 2lb/32oz lightly oiled and floured loaf tin (pan). Cover loosely with oiled foil and leave to rise until dough reaches top of tin (pan). Uncover.

6 Bake 25 to 30 minutes in oven preheated to 230C/450F/Gas 8 when loaf should look golden brown and crusty. If it begins to darken too much, cover with a piece of foil during last 10 minutes of baking. Leave until lukewarm (tepid) then turn out and cool on wire rack. Store in a bread bin for 2-3 days when cold.

Barley bread

MAKES 1 LOAF

Healthily different.

350g/12oz/3 cups wholmeal flour (graham flour)
125g/4oz/³/₄ cup barley flour
¹/₂ tsp salt or substitute
1 sachet easy blend dried yeast
350ml/12 fluid oz/1 ¹/₂ cups lukewarm (tepid) water
2 tsp sunflower oil

1 Tip both flours into bowl then toss in salt and yeast.
2 Mix to dough with water and oil then turn out on to floured surface and knead 10 to 12 minutes until smooth and stretchy. If dough remains on the sticky side, work in a little extra wholemeal flour.
3 Transfer to clean and lightly oiled bowl, cover with oiled plastic wrap and leave dough to rise in a warm place - like an airing cupboard - for about 1¹/₂ hours or in the kitchen about 3 hours. Dough should double in size.
4 Return to floured work surface and quickly knead flat (known as punching down). Shape into an oblong and drop into a 1kg/2lb/32oz lightly oiled and floured loaf tin (pan). Cover loosely with oiled foil and leave to rise in the warm until dough reaches top of tin (pan).
5 Bake 25 minutes in oven preheated to 230C/450F/Gas 8. Cool 10 minutes then turn out on to wire rack. Store in a bread bin when cold.

Gerald's rye and fennel bread

MAKES 1 LOAF

Gerald is a cousin and a chemist, now turned bread buff. This is my version of one of his recipes which can best be described as true Continental with its beige colour, texture and pronounced taste of fennel. It's made for Med food and oily fish dishes and should be left one day before cutting.

225g/8oz/about 1 $\frac{3}{4}$ to 2 cups rye flour
225g/8oz/2 cups strong white plain flour (all-purpose)
1 tsp salt or substitute
2 to 3 tsp fennel seeds
1 sachet easy blend dried yeast
350ml/12 fluid oz/1 $\frac{1}{2}$ cups lukewarm (tepid) water
1 tbsp sunflower oil

1 Tip rye flour into mixing bowl then sift in white flour and salt.
2 Toss in fennel seeds and yeast then mix to dough with water and oil. Turn out on to floured surface and knead 10 to 12 minutes until smooth, elastic and no longer sticky. If need be, work in a little more white flour.
3 Return to a clean and lightly oiled bowl, cover with oiled plastic wrap and leave in the kitchen to rise until double in size; anything from 3 to 5 hours depending on temperature of room. Gerald says he goes away and forgets about it for a good half a day but if you want the whole thing over and done with more quickly, leave to rise in a warm place like an airing cupboard for about 1 $\frac{1}{2}$ to 2 hours.
4 Return to floured surface and quickly knead flat (known as punching down). Shape into an oblong and drop into a lightly oiled and floured 1kg/2lb/32oz loaf tin (pan). Cover loosely with oiled foil and leave to rise until dough reaches top of tin (pan). Uncover.

5 Bake 25 minutes in hot oven set to 230C/450F/Gas 8. Cool 10 minutes then turn out on to a wire rack. Store in a bread bin when cold.

Rye and aniseed bread

Substitute aniseeds for the fennel.

Brown soda bread

MAKES 1 LOAF

Dense and full of wheaten flavour, traditional bread like this can be prepared speedily and takes only half an hour to bake. It holds up well in a plastic bag in the fridge and responds favourably to toasting. It's based on an old Irish recipe and in case buttermilk is not readily available where you live, make a fair copy by lightly whisking together equal amounts of low fat yogurt and skimmed milk.

150g/5oz/⁵⁄₈ cup low fat yogurt
150ml/5 fluid oz/⁵⁄₈ cup skimmed milk
2 tbsp sunflower oil
350g/12oz/3 cups wholemeal flour (graham flour)
125g/4oz/1 cup plain white flour (all-purpose)
1 tsp bicarbonate of soda
1 tsp baking powder
6 tbsp sparkling mineral water

1 Set oven to 220C/425F/Gas 7. Lightly oil and flour a baking tray (cookie sheet).
2 Beat together yogurt, milk and oil.
3 Tip wholemeal flour into mixing bowl then sift in white flour with bicarbonate of soda and baking powder.
4 Fork in yogurt mixture and mineral water to form a soft dough.
5 Turn out on to floured surface and knead quickly and lightly until smooth.
6 Shape into 20cm/8-inch round and transfer to prepared tin. Score a cross on top with knife to make 4 quarters.
7 Bake 30 minutes. Cool 10 minutes then transfer to wire rack. Break into 4 sections when just cold. Store in bread bin or in plastic bag in the fridge.

CAKES

Prune and banana cake

MAKES 1 FAMILY SIZE CAKE

The Californian Prune people have come up with a seemingly helpful and clever idea though it does demand a sturdy blender for success. Prunes puréed with water, they say, make an ideal substitute for fat in baking, doing away with pangs of guilt every time you bite into a slice of cake. I partially subscribe to their theory but found it necessary to add two tablespoons of oil to the mixture to make the texture moist and tender. The cake turns out to be one of those cut and come again efforts associated with old-fashioned home baking and afternoon tea or mid-morning coffee round the kitchen table and if it isn't featherlight, it has other qualities to recommend it - it's nourishing, easy to make, keeps well tightly foil-wrapped in the fridge and has a nice taste.

125g/4oz/prunes without stones (pitted)
3 tbsp water
350g/12oz/3 cups self-raising flour
125g/4oz/$\frac{1}{2}$ cup light brown sugar
1 large egg, beaten
2 tbsp sunflower oil
1 large peeled and mashed banana
1 tsp vanilla essence (extract)
150ml/$\frac{1}{4}$ pt/$\frac{5}{8}$ cup skimmed milk

1 Lightly oil a 1kg/2lb/32oz loaf tin (pan) then line base and sides with non-stick parchment paper. If tin (pan) is non-stick, line base only. Set oven to 180C/350F/ Gas 4.
2 Snip prunes into pieces with kitchen scissors and blend with water to smooth purée in blender. Scrape out into mixing bowl.
3 Add all remaining ingredients and fork-stir until well-combined.
4 Transfer to prepared tin (pan) and bake for 1 hour until well-risen and golden brown. Cool on wire rack then store airtight.

Nut and raisin cake

MAKES 1 FAMILY SIZE CAKE

A fairly plain and lightly sweetened yeasted cake which can be sliced and spread with jam or thick flowery honey or, for those with a penchant for savouries, with cottage cheese or crunchy peanut butter.

450g/1lb/4 cups strong plain flour (all-purpose)
1 tsp salt or substitute
1 sachet easy blend dried yeast
75g/3oz/$\frac{1}{2}$ cup raisins
50g/2oz/$\frac{1}{4}$ cup chopped (minced) walnuts
75g/3oz/$\frac{3}{8}$ cup caster (superfine) sugar
1 tbsp sunflower oil
275ml/$\frac{1}{2}$ pt/1 $\frac{1}{4}$ cups skimmed milk, just warm

1 Oil a 450g/1lb/16oz loaf tin (pan) and line with non-stick parchment paper. If tin (pan) itself is non-stick, line base only.
2 Sift flour and salt into mixing bowl. Toss in yeast, raisins, nuts and sugar.
3 Mix to dough with oil and milk then turn out on to lightly floured surface. Knead 10 to 12 minutes until smooth and elastic, working in a little extra flour if dough stays on the wet side.
4 Return to clean and lightly-oiled bowl and cover with oiled plastic wrap. Leave in warm place to rise (an airing cupboard or above an Aga) until dough doubles in size, allowing between 1 and 2 hours.
5 Return to floured work surface and quickly knead flat (known as punching down). Shape into oblong and drop into tin (pan). Cover with oiled foil and leave to rise until dough reaches top of tin.
6 Bake 40 minutes in oven prehated to 220C/425F/Gas 7. Turn out and cool on wire rack. Eat as fresh as possible, storing leftovers in airtight container.

Barm brack

MAKES 1 CAKE

An Irish speciality, made with oil instead of the more customary lard, margarine or butter. Heavily fruited and spiked with whiskey (or whisky!), it makes a highly acceptable Christmas cake and responds excellently to deep-freezing if you want to bake ahead of time.

150g/5oz/⅝ cup light brown soft sugar (muscovado or coffee sugar)
275ml/½ pt/1¼ cups hot strong tea, strained
450g/16oz/just over 3 cups mixed dried fruits including peel (candied peel)
50ml/2 fluid oz/¼ cup sunflower oil
1 large egg, beaten
50g/2oz/⅜ cup glacé (candied) cherries, roughly chopped
25g/1oz/¼ cup walnuts or pecans, roughly chopped
275g/10oz/2½ cups plain white flour (all-purpose flour)
3 tsp baking powder
3 tbsp whisky (whisky or bourbon)

1 Put sugar into large bowl, add tea and stir until melted. Add fruit and peel and well mix in. Cover with plate or a piece of foil and leave to stand overnight.
2 Oil and line a 20cm/8 inch deep round cake tin (pan). Set oven to 180C/350F/Gas 4.
3 Stir oil and egg into fruit mixture with cherries and nuts. Sift flour and baking powder over the top and gently fork in.
4 When evenly-combined, spread smoothly into prepared tin and bake for 1¼ to 1½ hours until well-risen and golden brown. If top darkens too much, cover lightly with a piece of foil towards the end of baking.
5 To check if cake is ready, push a skewer gently into centre. If it comes out cleanly with no uncooked mixture sticking to it,

the cake has been baked long enough. If not, cook a further 10 minutes or so.

6 Remove from oven and pour whisky over the top. Give it time to soak in, allowing about 30 minutes. Turn cake out on to a wire cooling rack and turn right way up when cold. Over wrap with greaseproof (waxed) paper followed by foil. Store in the cool and leave at least 1 week before cutting.

Honey spice-cake

MAKES 1 FAMILY SIZE CAKE

Imagine a cake that's so light and so tender, it almost floats; a cake with a distinct buttery taste yet is made with the lightest of oils; a cake that adapts happily to conventional baking or a stint in the microwave; a cake that freezes so perfectly leftovers are never wasted. You can't better it, that's for sure but you will need a food processor to make it properly or an electric mixer with a large bowl like the new Kitchen Aid.

3 tbsp orange or ginger marmalade (conserve/preserve)
225g/8oz/1 cup clear honey
2 medium eggs
120ml/4 fluid oz/$^1\!/_2$ cup sunflower oil
150ml/$^1\!/_4$ pt/$^5\!/_8$ cup warm water
250g/9oz/just over 2 cups self-raising flour
1 tsp bicarbonate of soda (baking soda)
2 tsp ground ginger
2 tsp allspice or mixed spice
2 tsp ground cinnamon

1 Tip marmalade, honey, eggs, oil and water into food processor bowl. Cover. Whizz round for a few seconds until well-combined.
2 Sift together dry ingredients. With machine switched off, spoon gradually into bowl. Cover again and run machine until mixture looks like golden-coloured cream - really smooth.
3 For conventional baking, pour into a 20cm/8-inch round cake tin lined with non-stick parchment paper. Bake until well-risen and golden brown, allowing 1 to 1$^1\!/_4$ hours in oven preheated to 160C/325F/Gas 3. To test if ready, push a fine skewer gently into centre of cake. If it comes out clean and dry, the cake is ready. If not, return to oven and cook an extra 10

minutes. Switch off heat and leave cake in the oven to rest 15minutes.

4 Cool to lukewarm (tepid) then turn out on a wire rack. Store airtight when cold.

For microwave cooking:
Pour mixture into a 1^{3}/$_{4}$ litre /3pint/7^{1}/$_{2}$ cups deep round souffle dish first closely lined with plastic wrap. Bake for 10 to 10^{1}/$_{2}$ minutes at full power in a 650 watt oven. Cake is ready when it is well-risen and the top peppered with small air holes. Cool in dish then lift out by holding wrap. Transfer to wire rack and peel away wrap when cake is cold.

Note:
If using an electric cake mixer, put all the liquidy first five ingredients into bowl first. Beat gently with beaters until well-mixed. Gradually add sifted dry ingredients. When smoothly mixed in, increase speed and beat 5 minutes. Bake convention-ally or in the microwave.

Blueberry and vanilla muffins

MAKES 10

Low fat cakes from the USA which are fast catching on over here. They're akin to fairy cakes but bigger and squashier.

250g/9oz/2$\frac{1}{4}$ cups plain white flour (all-purpose)
2 tsp baking powder
65g/2$\frac{1}{2}$ oz/just over $\frac{1}{4}$ cup caster (superfine) sugar
125g/4oz/1 cup fresh or frozen blueberries, thawed
1 medium egg
175ml/6 fluid oz/$\frac{3}{4}$ cup skimmed milk
1 tsp vanilla essence (extract)
50ml/2 fluid oz/$\frac{1}{4}$ cup sunflower oil

1 Set oven to 200C/400F/Gas 6. Put 10 large paper cake cases into 10 large bun tins (muffin pans) or use standard size paper cases placed in 14 tins/pans.
2 Sift flour and baking powder into bowl. Toss in sugar and blueberries.
3 Beat egg and milk well together then stir in vanilla and oil.
4 Add to flour mixture in one go and stir round quickly, without beating, until barely mixed - consistency should be lumpy.
5 Spoon into paper cases and bake large muffins for 20 minutes, smaller ones for about 12 to 15 minutes. When cooked, muffins should be light golden brown, well-risen and cracked a little on top.
6 Cool on wire rack and store in plastic bag in the fridge when cold. Warm through before eating.

Tip
If stored in a cake tin, the fruit will turn mouldy. The best place is the fridge.

♥

Apple and blackberry cinnamon muffins

Make as above, sifting 2 teaspoons cinnamon with dry ingredients. Omit blueberries, substituting 50g/2oz/$\frac{1}{2}$ cup black-berries and 1 medium peeled and grated dessert apple.

VEGETABLE DISHES AND SALADS

Mixed mushroom stir-fry with tofu and spring onions

SERVES 3 TO 4

This, and the following recipe, have been adapted from ones which first appeared in the book I wrote called The Low Cholesterol Glutton, *published in 1990. They both feature tofu, a curd-like, high-protein product made from soy-beans which is bland of itself but picks up flavours from any other stronger ingredients with which it is combined.*

275g/300g/10 to 11oz mixed fresh mushrooms
1 small onion
1 tbsp peanut (groundnut) oil
1 pkt (284g/10oz) tofu, plain or smoked and drained
1 tbsp cornflour (cornstarch)
2 tbsp ginger wine or ginger syrup
1 tbsp soy sauce
5 tbsp water
$^1\!/_2$ tsp salt or substitute
$^1\!/_4$ tsp chilli sauce

1 Trim and wash mushrooms then wipe dry with paper towels. Fairly thinly slice.
2 Peel onion, cut into thin slices then separate slices into rings.
3 Heat oil until sizzling in a wok or large frying pan. Add onion and stir-fry fairly briskly for 1 minute. Add mushrooms and continue to stir-fry for 3 minutes. Take wok or pan off heat.
4 Cut tofu into small cubes. Mix cornflour (cornstarch) smoothly with all remaining ingredients.
5 Add tofu and cornflour (cornstarch) mixture to mushrooms. Stir-fry fairly quickly until liquid bubbles and thickens, allowing 2 to 3 minutes.

Mixed vegetable stir-fry with tofu and courgette (zucchini)

SERVES 4

1 packet (284g/10oz) tofu, drained
175g/6oz Chinese leaves (pak-choy)
8 button mushrooms
1 small red pepper (bell pepper)
1 tbsp peanut (groundnut) oil
175g/6oz bean sprouts
8 baby sweetcorn, fresh or canned
1 clove of garlic, peeled and crushed
12 walnut halves, chopped coarsely
1 tbsp cornflour (cornstarch)
4 tbsp cold water
2 tsp soy sauce
2 tsp Worcester sauce
1 tbsp medium sherry
$\frac{1}{2}$ tsp salt or substitute

1 Cut tofu into small cubes. Wash and drain Chinese leaves and finely shred. Thinly slice mushrooms. Wash, dry and halve pepper then remove inside fibres and seeds. Cut flesh into narow strips.
2 Heat oil in a wok until sizzling. Add all prepared vegetables followed by bean sprouts, sweetcorn, garlic and nuts. Stir-fry 8 minutes.
3 Add tofu and stir-fry gently a further 2 minutes. To thicken, mix cornflour (cornstarch) with all remaining ingredients.
4 Pour into tofu mixture and stir-fry, tossing gently, until ingredients are glossy and liquid thickened. Serve straight away with freshly cooked noodles.

Spicy vegetable kebabs

SERVES 4

A lively mix of vegetables on sticks in a peanut butter marinade was inspired by Schwartz, known for herbs and spices on both sides of the Atlantic. The kebabs are perfect for the barbecue and will make any vegetarian happy.

1kg/2lb/32oz mixed vegetables to include aubergine (egg plant), courgettes (zucchini), cherry tomatoes, button mushrooms, red or green pepper (bell pepper) and par-boiled small new potatoes.

<u>Marinade</u>
1 tbsp peanut (groundnut) oil
2 tbsp smooth peanut butter
1 tbsp soy sauce
Juice of 1 medium lemon
2 tsp caster (superfine) sugar
$\frac{1}{2}$ tsp EACH garlic granules, crushed chillies and ground cumin
1 tsp EACH ground coriander and oregano
6 tbsp canned coconut milk

1 Wash and dry raw vegetables (no need to do this to potatoes) and cut into bite-size cubes. Thread on to 4 long skewers, with potatoes.
2 For marinade, mix all ingredients well together, excluding coconut milk, and beat until smooth. Gradually whisk in coconut milk.
3 Arrange skewers in an oblong dish in a single layer. Coat with marinade. Leave to stand for 2 hours, turning skewers over several times.
4 Barbecue or grill for 15 minutes.

Sauerkraut salad with carrots and peppers

SERVES 4

A winter tonic, full of vitamins A and C, sparkling with vitality. Eat with poultry or meaty fish like mackerel, herring, tuna and pilchards.

228g/8oz/about 1 cup sauerkraut
1 medium green pepper (bell pepper)
2 medium carrots
1 small onion
2 tsp clear honey
1 tbsp sunflower oil

Garnish
Cress

1 Wash sauerkraut under cold running water and leave in colander to drain until almost dry. Fork round once or twice.
2 Wash, halve and dry pepper. Remove inside fibres and seeds then cut flesh into narrow strips. Peel and grate carrots. Peel onion, slice thinly then separate slices into rings.
3 Tip sauerkraut into large bowl. Add all remaining ingredients and toss with 2 forks until well-mixed. Transfer to salad bowl and garnish with cress.

Pumpernickel salad

SERVES 4

A healthy choice for summer if you appreciate off-beat flavours.

75g/3oz whole grain pumpernickel (sold in packets and often called
German black bread)
1 tbsp raspberry vinegar
1 $\frac{1}{2}$ tsp sesame oil
$\frac{1}{2}$ medium cucumber
275g/10oz/about 1 $\frac{1}{4}$ cups low fat cottage cheese
1 small lettuce heart
2 medium tomatoes
1 small carrot
2 tsp finely chopped (minced) parsley

1 Cut bread into small cubes and put into mixing bowl. Add
   vinegar and oil then leave to soak in while preparing
   remaining ingredients.
2 Wash and dry cucumber then cut into small cubes. Add to
   pumpernickel with cottage cheese. Toss well with 2 spoons.
3 Wash lettuce, shake dry and cut into shreds. Wash and dry
   tomatoes and cut into segments. Peel and grate carrot.
4 Line 4 individual bowls with shredded lettuce. Pile pumpernickel and cheese mixture on top.
5 Garnish each with tomatoes, carrot and parsley. Eat on its own
   with jacket potatoes or with hot roast turkey.

Apple and onion coleslaw

SERVES 4

A short-cut to crunch.

300g/11oz to 12oz pack of ready-prepared coleslaw mix
1 small onion
2 sweet dessert apples
8 tbsp low fat salad dressing (vinaigrette)
Salt or substitute and pepper to taste

1 Tip coleslaw mix into large mixing bowl.
2 Peel onion and finely grate. Wash and dry unpeeled apples then quarter and core. Roughly chop or grate flesh.
3 Add both to bowl with dressing and salt and pepper to taste. Toss thoroughly. Eat with almost anything.

Three cabbage slaw

SERVES 8 AT LEAST.

A vividly-coloured cabbage combination, charmed with a brand new spicy dressing.

225g/8oz/2$\frac{1}{2}$ cups EACH white, deep green Savoy and red cabbage

<u>Dressing</u>
2 tbsp tomato purée (paste)
1 tbsp tarragon vinegar
Juice of $\frac{1}{2}$ lemon
1 tsp sugar
$\frac{1}{2}$ tsp salt
4 tbsp carrot juice
5 tbsp chopped (minced) parsley
1$\frac{1}{2}$ tbsp olive oil

1 Remove outer leaves from cabbages and discard if they are bruised or damaged. Shred remainder finely with a sharp knife or in a food processor. Transfer to a roomy bowl.
2 Put all dressing ingredients into saucepan with the exception of last two. Slowly bring to boil, stirring.
3 Remove from heat and gently whisk in parsley and oil. Pour hot over cabbages and toss well together to mix. Cover and refrigerate 6 to 8 hours before eating.

Bean sprout and mushroom salad with lemon grass

SERVES 4

Crisp and fresh with a distinct taste of far away. Chicken loves it and so does baked or grilled fish.

175g/6oz bean sprouts
10 medium mushrooms
1 clove of garlic
2.5 to 3 cm/1 inch piece of fresh ginger
1 blade of lemon grass
1 tbsp peanut (groundnut) oil
1 tsp Worcester sauce
$\frac{1}{4}$ tsp salt

1 Rinse bean sprouts and drain thoroughly. Trim mushrooms and dice. Put both into a salad bowl.
2 Peel and crush garlic into small mixing bowl. Peel and finely chop ginger. Trim lemon grass and also finely chop. Mix all three together then finely grind in small food processor.
3 Return to bowl and beat in remaining ingredients. Toss with bean sprouts and mushrooms.

Green bean and water chestnut salad

SERVES 4

A side salad with bite and might for anyone who appreciates texture contrasts and a mildly fiery, pink-tinted dressing. As a matter of interest, water chestnuts are classed as a vegetable, not a nut, and are the small roots of water plants found in the Far East. Fresh ones are available but canned are easier to cope with.

300g/11oz to 12oz slender green beans like French or Kenyan
Boiling salted water
1 clove of garlic, peeled and halved
1 can (225g/about 8oz/1 cup) water chestnuts

<u>Dressing</u>
1 tsp powdered mustard
2 tsp tomato purée (paste)
1 tsp olive oil
2 tsp wine or cider vinegar
$\frac{1}{2}$ tsp caster sugar
$\frac{1}{2}$ tsp salt

1 Top and tail beans and rinse well. Cook in boiling salted water with the garlic until tender but still quite crisp. Strain and rinse under cold water.
2 Drain thoroughly and tip into a mixing bowl, discarding garlic. Drain water chestnuts and cut each into 3 pieces. Add to beans.
3 For dressing, beat all ingredients well together. Add to beans and chestnuts and toss thoroughly with 2 spoons.
4 Serve on side plates.

Chicory and cottage cheese salad with fruit and cress

SERVES 4

A bonanza of good things for healthy eating. To keep it all vegetarian, eat with freshly boiled new potatoes or brown soda bread (my recipe is on page 213). Otherwise have on the side with fish and poultry.

125g/4oz/about $^3/_4$ to 1 cup stoned (pitted) dates
1 green unpeeled dessert apple
1 red unpeeled dessert apple
2 heads Belgian chicory (endive)
1 box cress
200g/7oz/1 cup low fat cottage cheese
Salt or substitute and pepper to taste

1 Chop dates coarsely and put into bowl. Wash and dry both apples then peel, core and thinly slice. Add to dates.
2 Trim chicory and remove a cone-shaped core from base of each with a potato peeler to reduce bitterness. Thinly slice both heads with a stainless knife.
3 Rinse cress while still in its box. Shake dry and trim level to top of box. Add to dates and apples with chicory.
4 Stir in cottage cheese then season with salt and pepper to taste. Serve on 4 side plates.

Aubergine (eggplant) salad

SERVES 4

Something which originates from everywhere and anywhere where the sun shines down on familiar holiday spots - North Africa, the Middle East and Balkans. It's simple yet an acquired taste, a tour de force spread on to chunky slices of warm sesame seed bread or packed into warm pittas, a meal alone or an informal starter if you're eating outdoors.

2 medium aubergines (eggplants)
1 clove of garlic
1 tsp salt or substitute
Juice of ¹/₂ large lemon
3 medium tomatoes, blanched

1 Set oven to 190C/375F/Gas 9. Wash and dry aubergines (eggplant). Score a line lengthwise round the centre of each which will open up during baking and act as a cutting guide later on.
2 Put on to baking tray (cookie sheet) lined with foil, first lightly brushed with oil. Bake 45 minutes.
3 Remove from oven and leave until cool enough to handle. Halve each lengthwise along score line then remove flesh carefully with spoon. Tip into blender goblet.
4 Peel garlic and slice. Add to blender with salt and lemon juice and work to a fairly smooth purée. Scrape into bowl.
5 Peel and chop tomatoes. Stir into aubergine (eggplant) mixture then transfer to a serving dish.

Beetroot and banana salad

SERVES 2 TO 3

Firm beetroot and soft banana get together to make a merry salad of contrasts. Warmly recommended for grilled fish.

225g/8oz pickled beetroot (beets)
1 medium banana
1 small onion
75g/3oz/³/₈ cup low fat yogurt
3 fairly large mint leaves or 6 smaller ones, washed and dried
Salt or substitute to taste
Extra mint leaves for garnising

1 Drain beetroots (beets), cut into smallish cubes and put into mixing bowl. Slice in banana.
2 Peel and chop onion then stir into beetroot (beets) and banana with yogurt.
3 Cut first lot of mint leaves into shreds. Add to salad with salt and toss lightly to mix.
4 Transfer to serving dish and garnish with extra mint.

Cracked wheat salad

SERVES 6 TO 8

Also called burghul or bulgar, this Middle Eastern/North African salad is considered a smart thing to have about the place and goes with things like roast or grilled poultry and fish, egg concoctions and conventional salads. It's a buffet party must, all the rage in North France and has an earthiness and peasant quality about it that's all soul.

250g/9oz/1 ¼ cups cracked wheat
About ¾ litre/1 ½ pt/3 ¾ cups boiling water
1 ½ tsp salt or substitute
6 tbsp finely chopped (minced) fresh curly parsley
2 tbsp finely chopped (minced) mint
Juice of 1 small lemon
3 tsp olive oil
12 black olives without stones (pitted)
2 medium tomatoes
¼ unpeeled cucumber

1 Tip cracked wheat into large bowl and stir in water with salt. Cover with saucepan lid or plate and leave until cold.
2 Drain and transfer to mixing bowl. Stir in salt, parsley, mint, lemon juice and oil.
3 Halve olives. Wash and dry tomatoes and cucumber. Cut tomatoes into segments and cucumber into small cubes.
4 Put cracked wheat into salad bowl and garnish to taste with olives, tomatoes and cucumber.

Tarator

SERVES 6 TO 8

A Macedonian speciality based on cucumber, hotted up with chillies, calmed down with yogurt. It's sensational with freshly cooked baby new potatoes, roast chicken, grilled mackerel.

3 medium cucumbers
2 to 3 fresh green chillies
450g to 500g/1lb/2 cups Greek style low fat yogurt
2 to 3 cloves of garlic, peeled
Salt or substitute to taste

1 Wash unpeeled cucumbers, wipe dry and very thinly slice. Put into bowl, cover and leave to stand about $1\frac{1}{2}$ hours to give liquid time to leech out. Drain and wipe dry in clean towel. Return to washed and dried bowl.
2 Wash and dry chillies. slit each open and remove seeds. Cut flesh into hair thin strips and add to cucumber. Wash hands straight away to prevent skin burns.
3 Stir yogurt into cucumbers and chillies then crush in garlic. Add salt to taste and stir round until thoroughly mixed. Chill lightly before serving.

Salad niçoise

Serves 2

Another forgotten favourite from the South of France which contains all the elements of a well-balanced meal.

2 lettuce hearts or little gem lettuces
2 large tomatoes
225g/8oz/2 cups cooked potatoes, diced
225g/8oz/2 cups cooked green beans
5 tbsp low fat salad dressing like vinaigrette
1 can (200g/7oz/1 cup) tuna in olive oil
1 small can anchovy fillets in olive oil
12 small black olives
1 tbsp small size capers, drained

1 Wash lettuces and drain thoroughly then arrange leaves over base of a large serving plate or shallow dish.
2 Cut tomatoes downwards into segments (12 from each) and transfer to mixing bowl. Add potatoes, beans and about 3 tablespoons of dressing. Toss gently to mix.
3 Arrange in a mound over the lettuce. Divide tuna into large flakes and place on top of potato mixture. Trickle tuna oil from can over the top.
4 Garnish with anchovies, olives and capers then coat with remaining dressing. Serve at room temperature.

Fennel and orange salad

SERVES 4

An elusive-tasting salad based on one of Italy's most esteemed vegetables - Florence fennel. Teamed with orange and olives, it makes a pretty sight and the fact the the fennel's cooked in the microwave adds a practical high-speed dimension.

1 head of fennel
6 tbsp water
$\frac{1}{2}$ tsp salt or substitute
2 large oranges
12 black olives without stones (pitted)
3 tsp olive oil
1 $\frac{1}{2}$ tsp wine vinegar
Red-tipped lettuce such as lollo rosso

1 Trim fennel as little as possible and put into dish suitable for the microwave.
2 Add water and salt then cover with plastic wrap, slitting twice to allow steam to escape. Cook 8 minutes at full power in a 650 watt microwave. Stand for 10 minutes. Drain and cool.
3 Peel oranges, removing all traces of white pith. Thinly slice on board then cut each slice into 4 pieces. Tip into mixing bowl with juice.
4 Slice fennel thinly as you would an onion and separate slices into rings. Add to bowl with rest of ingredients (except lettuce) and toss lightly to mix.
5 Fringe 4 side plates with washed and dried lollo rosso lettuce leaves then fill centres with fennel and orange mixture.

Orange and tomato salad with pesto dressing

SERVES 4

A handsome and original tapestry of sweet-sour tastes and textures, the ideal companion for pasta and poultry.

3 medium oranges
3 medium tomatoes
3 tsp green pesto (basil sauce)
2 tsp balsamic vinegar
1 tsp icing (confectioner's) sugar
Fresh basil leaves for garnishing

1 Peel oranges, removing all traces of white pith. Put on to board then slice fairly thinly. Wash and dry tomatoes and also thinly slice.
2 Fill a large serving plate with alternate rings of oranges and tomatoes.
3 Beat pesto with vinegar and sugar. Spoon over salad and garnish with basil.

242

Broad bean and garlic salad with mixed herbs

SERVES 4 TO 6

You need time for this one because the beans are prepared in much the same way as they are in high-profile hotels - laboriously. But it's worth it and the salad makes a discreet addition to any buffet, summer or winter, and for any occasion. Personally, I believe frozen beans give the best results but if you grow your own, cook and use as you please.

1kg/2lb/32oz frozen broad beans, thawed
Boiling salted water
1 tsp chopped (minced) garlic, frozen or fresh
1 tbsp EACH chopped (minced) fresh or frozen curly parsley, flat parsley, marjoram and chives
1 tsp prepared mild mustard
1 tbsp sherry vinegar
2 tbsp olive oil
$\frac{1}{2}$ to 1 tsp salt or substitute
Leaves of oak leaf lettuce or radicchio for garnishing, washed and dried

1 Peel beans individually (a slow job) which will reveal a set of twins inside each like embyros. They will be vivid green. Separate each pair.
2 Cook for 3 minutes in boiling salted water. Drain thoroughly and tip into mixing bowl.
3 Combine all remaining ingredients, with the exception of lettuce, in a small bowl and beat until smoothly mixed.
4 Add to beans and toss gently to mix.
5 Transfer to serving dish and garnish with lettuce. Serve at room temperature.

Mediterranean bean salad

SERVES ABOUT 4 TO 6 AS A MAIN MEAL, 8 AS A STARTER

Cooked in the Swan Slow Cooker, the recipe comes from the company's home economics department and is a triumph of science! The beans, cloaked in a lemony dressing, can be eaten as a complete meal with rice or jacket potatoes and they also make an up-to-the-minute side dish, served at room temperature just as they are and eaten with crusty bread.

2 medium onions
2 cloves of garlic
3 tbsp olive oil
1 large lemon
1 can (400g/14oz/1$^{3}/_{4}$ cups) chopped tomatoes
2 tsp soft brown sugar
4 tsp freeze dried French fines herbes
1 tbsp fresh thyme leaves
2 tbsp tomato purée (paste)
Salt or substitute and freshly-milled pepper to taste
1 can (400g/14oz/1$^{3}/_{4}$ cups) EACH of the following beans: cannellini,
    flageolet, red kidney and chick peas (gabanzos)

1 Peel onions, very thinly slice then separate slices into rings. Peel and crush garlic.
2 Put both into frying pan with oil and fry over medium heat until light golden brown, stirring from time to time.
3 Meanwhile wash lemon thoroughly and wipe dry. Remove peel thinly with a potato peeler then halve fruit and squeeze out juice. Combine juice in bowl with tomatoes, sugar, fines herbes, thyme, tomato purée (paste) and seasoning to taste.
4 Add to frying pan with onions and garlic. Cook, stirring, until mixture begins to boil and bubble.
5 Drain beans and chick peas and tip into slow cooker. Stir in tomato mixture and lemon peel then stir round to combine.

Cover and cook on auto for 3 to 5 hours to give flavours time to meld and mature.

Terracotta chicken salad

SERVES 8

The salad, colourwise, sets out to be an edible replica of the local pottery one sees in Balkan and Southern European street markets; those deep orangey red affairs with multi-coloured borders or asplash with Van Gogh-like flowers in hot, intense colours. As for flavour, it's slightly sweet sour, a touch hot, Cointreauy.

1 can (400g/14oz) sweeet red peppers or pimientos (bell peppers)
1 can (300g/12oz) sliced carrots
2 tsp Worcester sauce
1 tsp brown sugar
100g/3 $\frac{1}{2}$ oz/$\frac{1}{2}$ cup low fat Greek style yogurt or light crème fraîche
2 to 3 tsp bottled horseradish sauce
5 sprigs of fresh oregano
Salt or substitute to taste
1 clove of garlic, peeled and crushed
1 $\frac{1}{2}$ tbsp Cointreau
About 700g/1 $\frac{1}{2}$ lb/24oz cold cooked chicken
Inside leave of a cos (romaine) lettuce heart
16 black olives without stones (pitted)

1 Drain peppers and carrots, reserving liquid for soups or stews. Tip vegetables into blender goblet with next 8 ingredients. Run machine until mixture forms a smooth, purée-like dressing. Scrape into mixing bowl.
2 Cut chicken into smallish cubes. Add to dressing and toss gently with spoon until every piece is thoroughly coated.
3 Line a shallowish serving dish with washed and dried lettuce leaves. Fill with chicken mixture and garnish with olives.

Club salad

SERVES 4

Immersed in a snow storm of cottage cheese, try this USA style salad made from low fat smoked turkey (strips), the newest alternative to bacon. Eat with toasted muffins.

6 turkey rashers (strips)
1 small webb lettuce
225g/8oz/2 cups cooked potatoes, cut into small cubes
50g to 60g/2oz/$\frac{1}{2}$ cup garlic croutons
225g/8oz/1 cup low fat cottage cheese
1 box cress, washed and drained

1 Grill or fry turkey rashers (strips) as directed on packet. Cool and cut into squares.
2 Wash and dry lettuce then finely shred. Put into large mixing bowl.
3 Add potatoes, turkey, croutons and cottage cheese. Toss well to mix, transfer to serving dish and sprinkle with cress.

Club salad sandwich

EACH SANDWICH MAKES A MEAL FOR 1

Sandwich together two large slices of white or brown bread with the Club Salad above. Spread top of sandwich thinly with low fat mayonnaise or salad cream, cover with a large sliced tomato and top with third slice of bread. Press down firmly and cut into 2 triangles.

♥

Caesar's scallop salad

SERVES 4

A recipe to make expensive scallops go as far as they can. The little ones, a speciality of Britain's Isle of Man, are known as queenies. Large ones are just called scallops. Both are one of the most delicate, succulent and creamy-tasting shellfish the world over.

1 small crisp lettuce
228g/8oz scallops
150ml/$^1/_4$ pt/$^5/_8$ cup white wine or water
6 tbsp low fat salad dressing
2 cloves of garlic, peeled and crushed
2 tsp mild mustard
1 tsp brown sugar
Salt or substitute to taste
4 tbsp garlic croutons

1 Wash and dry lettuce then cut into fairly fine shreds. Arrange over bases of 4 side plates.
2 Rinse scallops gently then cut white flesh into slices and orange roes in half.
3 Poach for no longer than 2 to 3 minutes in wine or water. Lift out of pan on to plate lined with paper towels.
4 Put salad dressing into small mixing bowl. Add garlic, mustard, sugar and salt then beat together until well-mixed.
5 Arrange scallops and croutons on lettuce-lined plates and coat with garlic dressing. Serve straight away.

Note
Adapted from a recipe supplied by the Sea Fish Industry Authority of Edinburgh.

Chicken salad with tofu and teryaki dressing

SERVES 3 TO 4

A salad mix with a familiar waft of oriental aromas. Eat with wedges of brown bread or rolls.

140g/5oz tofu, drained
125g/4oz cooked smoked chicken slices
(from delicatessens and some supermarkets)
225g/8oz cherry tomatoes
1 smallish green-skinned apple
125g/4oz celery
2 knobs preserved ginger in syrup
1 tbsp teriyaki sauce (Japanese, sold in bottles)
2 tbsp red wine raspberry vinegar
1 garlic clove, peeled and crushed
lettuce leaves

1 Cut tofu into small cubes and put into bowl. Cut chicken into strips and add.
2 Halve tomatoes. Leave apple unpeeled then quarter, core and dice flesh into same sized pieces as the tofu. Cut celery diagonally into thin strips and coarsely chop ginger. Add all to bowl.
3 Beat teriyaki sauce with vinegar and garlic. Add to salad and gently stir round.
4 Cover and leave to stand at kitchen temperature for about 2 hours so that flavours have time to meld together.
5 To serve, spoon into little bowls lined with lettuce.

Fruited poultry and nut salad

Interesting this and another useful way of using up leftover poultry. Eat with hot toast.

225g/8oz cold cooked poultry - chicken, turkey, pheasant, etc.
white part of small leek
50g/2oz radishes
125g/4oz peeled and diced fresh orange
1 slice brown toast, cubed
8 to 9 tbsp light salad dressing
radicchio leaves
watercress or 8 lightly cooked mange tout

1 Cut poultry into small cubes and put into mixing bowl
2 Shred leek finely. Trim and thinly slice radishes. Add both to the poultry.
3 Mix in orange, toast and dressing then toss gently to mix.
4 Arrange on plates, the centres lined with raddichio leaves. Garnish with sprigs of watercress or mange tout. Eat soon to prevent toast cubes from becoming soggy.

INDEX

♥

♥